IF PACKAGING COULD TALK

unwrap the untapped value in your packaging for lasting **brand success**

KERAN TURAKHIA

RETHINK PRESS

First published in Great Britain 2017
by Rethink Press (www.rethinkpress.com)

© Copyright Keran Turakhia

All rights reserved. No part of this publication may be reproduced, stored in or introduced into a retrieval system, or transmitted, in any form, or by any means (electronic, mechanical, photocopying, recording or otherwise) without the prior written permission of the publisher.

The right of Keran Turakhia to be identified as the author of this work has been asserted by him in accordance with the Copyright, Designs and Patents Act 1988.

This book is sold subject to the condition that it shall not, by way of trade or otherwise, be lent, resold, hired out, or otherwise circulated without the publisher's prior consent in any form of binding or cover other than that in which it is published and without a similar condition including this condition being imposed on the subsequent purchaser.

CONTENTS

Foreword   7

Introduction   9

Chapter 1
THE BRAND MARKET THROUGH THE EYES OF A PACK   15

1. The grocery market   15
2. Retail stockists   18
3. Consumers   19
4. Media landscape   23
5. Retail landscape   27
6. Consumer engagement   28

Chapter 2
PACKAGING'S DAY JOB   33

Hold and protect the product   33
Advertise the brand   34
Describe the product   34
Make an impact   35
Packaging construction   37

Packaging design and print 54

Packaging texture 57

Packaging innovation: four common challenges 58

Chapter 3
PACKAGING MEDIA 63
Constructional mechanics 69

Mechanics with extra independent space 77

Where is the media value? 79

Proving packaging's media value 84

Chapter 4
PACKAGING'S DIGITAL MEDIA VALUE 95
The birth of smart connectable packaging 98

Coinks™ 99

The lesson in 'seeds' 104

Chapter 5
THE 6 RS METHODOLOGY 117
React 119

Read 126

Respond 134

Return	138
Remember	143
Recommend	146

Chapter 6
IMPLEMENTATION 153

Step 1: internal value metrics	154
Step 2: agreeing yardsticks	154
Step 3: assess packaging	155
Step 4: pilot study test	156
Step 5: implement	156
Step 6: ongoing assessment	156
Market for FMCG brands	157

Conclusion	*161*
Acknowledgements	*163*
About The Author	*165*

FOREWORD

When I was young, I was told by my teachers that I was not creative, simply because I was not good at art or playing the piano. For years, I believed what my teachers had told me.

However, in business, just as in every walk of life, you need to be creative if you want to succeed. To win a customer's attention, you have to stand out where no one else does.

When I started Cobra Beer, the branding was very important. I knew that the product was good – it was brewed to an innovative recipe that ensured a great taste was matched with a smooth and refreshing texture, so that the beer was the perfect accompaniment for any food. But the branding was what would get the beer noticed. Sitting at a table in a restaurant with a plain bottle of water and a Cobra Beer side-by-side, people will notice the Cobra Beer bottle. It has a striking design with bold colours and intricate scenes moulded on to the sides of the bottle, selling a story to anyone who sees the product even out of the corner of their eye.

Customers know the difference between the mundane and the extraordinary. To engage with a consumer market, you need to tell them a story or show them how complex, entertaining and curious the world can be. This takes creativity. Bringing Cobra Beer's packaging to life, I realised that creativity means more than practising scales on a piano or talent with a brush on canvas.

Keran Turakhia has turned that realisation into an exact study. His book, *If Packaging Could Talk*, will, I'm sure, inspire a more creative look at packaging and its central role in brand building. Everyone has a creative part of them, and the key is to be as creative as possible with your packaging. Use it to start a strong relationship with your consumer. Tell a story. *If Packaging Could Talk* puts a science to the creative process of packaging as a vital method to build a brand. It shows how packaging's communicative value can be taken to a new level.

Lord Karan Bilimoria CBE, DL
Founder of Cobra Beer, Chairman of the Cobra Beer Partnership Limited and Molson Coors Cobra India

INTRODUCTION

I frequently get accused of having a unique attitude and a different way of looking at things. I guess this comes from my unusual background, upbringing and education. My mother is half-English, half Swiss-German, and she married an Indian businessman. I was born in India, brought up amongst a handful of eccentric but special people, and educated alongside a range of different nationalities with different cultures and perspectives. The skill I developed of looking at things in a different way has been a cornerstone in my working life and has certainly helped me write this book.

Back in the 90s I was selling packaging and I was frustrated. However much effort and innovation I brought to a client, it was exceptionally difficult to make any serious money out of it. I would spend an enormous amount of energy and resource developing a new pack that would help my client sell his or her product, but once it was launched, the market would flood with alternative packaging suppliers wanting to manufacture similar designs. The inevitable result would be that a unique package quickly became commoditised and devalued, making it almost impossible to earn any significant margin from supplying it.

Around the same time, my wife asked whether she and the children could move to Spain for the summer months. I was not in a position to work away from the UK, but not being the type to let practicalities stop me doing something, I looked at the feasibility of moving my young family to Spain and flying over for the weekends. Though it sounded impossible, I was surprised to find a solution in easyJet which had just begun to provide low-cost flights from Luton to Barcelona. Miraculously, we could manage it, and we did.

So, what's that got to do with writing a book on packaging? Well, it was on one of those easyJet flights that I thought, *How can Stelios* [the founder of easyJet] *make money when he hardly charges anything?*

I learnt that he had developed a commercial model that wasn't completely reliant on the revenue from the seats. In fact, it was earning from the footfall custom resulting from the number of passengers his company channelled through airports like Stansted and Luton. This innovative non-linear model had proved hugely successful both for easyJet and the airports it employed. So, if Stelios could do it with airline tickets, what could I do with packaging?

I asked myself, 'Could packaging have a value that is not obvious and has not yet been commercially exploited?'

More than ten years later, having set up a company called Packaging Media Ltd, I have enough experience and real case studies to write a book on the hidden value of branded packaging. The new world is about sharing the experiences we have had for the greater good, so this book aims to look at packaging from a new perspective. If packaging could talk and justify its role to the brand it belongs to, what would it be saying? How could it help the brand to confront some of its main problems?

Introduction

This book shares a unique perspective on the challenge of adding value to packaging. I hope that it will help more brands look at their packaging in a different way and grow as a result. It is not a series of opinions and creative suggestions that I have concocted by looking at other brands' packs. Rather, it is a real life account of a business created around the media value of packaging and the potential untapped profit that can flow as a result of this media. It provides a simple methodology called the 6 Rs: six recommendations or rules to use when designing and evaluating the value of FMCG packaging.

I landed into packaging by chance, having studied Chemical Engineering and Management, but what fun it has been. From glueing up mini CD wallets to supplying Playtex bra cartons, selling decorated toilet rolls as fragrance boxes, printing unique codes on billions of crisp packets, I have never had a dull moment. Over the years I have learnt to see every box as untapped media value ready to be released.

Packaging should never be underestimated or undervalued. Indeed, as market technology grows, successfully exploiting a pack's media potential is more crucial for long lasting brand success. Packaging permits multiple direct consumer-to-brand connections, helping build strong relationships. Increasingly, these relationships are safeguarding a brand's price premium.

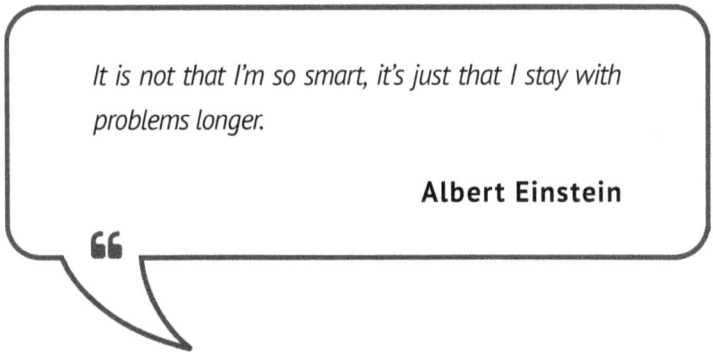

It is not that I'm so smart, it's just that I stay with problems longer.

Albert Einstein

Are you getting the most value from your packaging? It's well worth taking Einstein's advice and staying with it for longer.

Many thanks for picking this book up and I hope you find it of value.

Introduction

Packaging has to work even harder in future by offering benefits in and after use to manufacturers, its customers, end users and recyclers.

Matthew Daniels
Global Artwork Innovation Manager, Unilever
(Disclaimer: this is Matthew's personal opinion and not necessarily Unilever's)

Primary Packaging will empower the consumer in ways previously unimagined. To be able to interact with the product through the packaging will inform, entertain and encourage them to develop a relationship with the brand as well as offering safeguards. Smart packaging can change the way people think about its place in the value chain, revolutionizing the role it plays. It won't just talk, it will shout!

Eef de Ferrante
Executive Director, AIPIA (Active Intelligent Packaging Industry Association)

Chapter 1

THE BRAND MARKET THROUGH THE EYES OF A PACK

Imagine that a pack could talk. What would it be saying?

Packaging is typically defined and specified by its brand owners, often with scant consideration of actual consumer behaviour. In an attempt to think differently, this chapter looks at the world in which customers operate through the eyes of the packaging. It might come across a little like *Toy Story* at first, but hopefully it will help kick start the process of approaching packaging differently.

Here are six things the packs would likely be commenting on.

1. The grocery market

Wow, it's getting hard out there. There used to be a time when I was the leading product in my sector, but now there's so much competition. Everyone is trying to eat my lunch. Plus, the amount of copying – everyone is copying my design, trying to look just like me and then charging the customer much less. Don't the customers realise that they are being cheated? They aren't getting the real McCoy. It really is annoying.

Brand, customers are not listening to us anymore. We spend so much money on advertising on TV and radio. Can't we find a new way to get to them? They need to understand that they are not buying the same thing when they buy cheap imitations. We have spent time on developing our products and making sure that they are the best, yet customers simply go for the newcomers on the shelves, or compromise on price. Are times that tough out there? Can't they afford us? Why aren't they buying us as frequently?

We can't afford to sit on our laurels. Wish we could talk with our customers and really understand what they want and why.

> *Brands are in decline. According to an Ogilvy study, 77% of UK consumers claim that brands don't matter to them. In fact, 75% of brands are so meaningless to people that they wouldn't miss those brands if they disappeared tomorrow. Brands are no longer a proxy for quality.*
>
> **Mick Mahoney**
> Chief Creative Officer, Ogilvy & Mather

The Brand Market Through The Eyes Of A Pack

Times are changing fast, and consumers are not the same as they were. Competition is much more intense. There are two million more brands than there were in the year 2000.

2. Retail stockists

Shops – we seem to spend all our lives here. We never know where we are going to be located. Is it fair to put us on shelves next to a product that looks very similar to us, but costs much less? Is that allowed? Why can retailers' own brands blatantly copy our success? I am not sure I trust them. Are they getting too strong?

3. Consumers

What are our consumers into? I would love to ask them. They seem to be completely preoccupied with smartphones. What are they doing on their phones? How does the retailer know what they are up to? How do the retailers get to know them?

There's a lot of talk about the retail loyalty cards. Is this a way for the retailer to find out more about the consumers? They certainly seem to launch new products in our sector quickly and the consumers want them.

I would love a way to understand our consumers. I feel as if our relationship is getting weaker.

If Packaging Could Talk

Every three to four years I get a new design. Sometimes my shape and material is changed, but this is rare. Consumers like to feel informed and know what they are buying. They are usually more comfortable when they understand what my product is. That's why I am always nervous when I have had a redesign, hoping the consumers still recognise me.

Typically, my brand advertises me as much as possible, telling the prospective consumers why I am worth the price they sell me for. Sometimes the brand runs me on campaigns called 'price promotions', selling me at a reduced price. For a short period of time I get a lot more notice in the shops because of the low price I am being sold for.

But I am not sure how much damage price promotions do to me. I'm not a fan. They make me feel cheap and undervalued, but apparently they please our retail customers.

Here are the steps a typical customer goes through from my eyes.

Step 1: The consumer walks down the aisle that I am stocked in. Hopefully they will notice me and buy me.

Step 2: Often the consumer hovers around the shelf, looking at me and my competitors. This is when I am hoping my design stands out and consumers choose me. Usually shoppers are looking at the fact I'm more expensive than my competitors. It seems like an age before they make their mind up. I wish I could speak, dance or move – anything to persuade them to pick me.

I remember the days when shoppers never hovered; they just picked me up and moved on. The hover phase is getting longer and is really painful – it can take up to five minutes. It's enough to give me a complex.

It's a tough business being a pack. We have to have really thick skins, otherwise we would be constantly depressed.

Step 3: The customer buys me. A feeling of relief. I can relax now as I will soon be scanned and tossed into a shopping bag, but this is getting rarer.

Step 4: I am in my new home, being unpacked and put away. This is usually nice as my new owner picks me up, touches me, reads my information, turns me around. Away from the busy shopping aisles, into the warmth and comfort of a kitchen, I seem to be treated with more respect. I get most of my love and attention at this stage. It's flattering. I think I have my customer's attention here.

Step 5: The customer uses my product. Often, they'll read my information again and look at me while they're preparing the product, and then they'll throw me, the package, away.

My relationship with my customer is short, but worthwhile. The journey my customer takes from getting to know my brand to buying me and using me is called the 'path to purchase'. I think we should add 'post-purchase' and 'use' as well, as these are often the best times I experience with my customers.

We need to study the journey our customers take from buying me and using me.

The Brand Market Through The Eyes Of A Pack

4. Media landscape

The advertising landscape has completely changed for me. I remember a time when my brand would simply run a strong advertising campaign on TV and radio and that would be enough for consumers to buy me and stay loyal. This is no longer the case.

The media landscape is now much more fragmented and difficult. 'Media proliferation' it's called – the explosion of media channels. If I was a consumer, I would be suffering from information fatigue. They are bombarded with messages from a large number of channels, there are lots more advertising choices for brands to spend their money on, and it's not that clear which channel will deliver the results needed. Consumers have access to more information and hence are less reliant on brands as a source of information. Brand communication has to go deeper than the traditional 'media bribe'.

> *The only way for brands to stand out and remain memorable is to live inside the real-world conversations their customers are having.*
>
> **Mick Mahoney**
> Chief Creative Officer, Ogilvy & Mather

It can't be easy for brand marketers to get the ear of target consumers. The increased competition on the shelf is really making it a hostile environment out there. All the media experts talk about 'relevance' – finding a subject relevant enough to make the consumer want to engage. One-off connections are not sufficient; brands need a deeper, more meaningful relationship with their consumer. And all this before the consumer buys the product.

Even though there is an increased number of media solutions, media prices are still high and brands can't keep spending without a clear indication of a return on investment (ROI). On top of conventional media – TV, radio, online and print, retailers are putting pressure on my brand to spend on their media. My brand has to shell out for posters in store, adverts on the back of the till receipt, floor signs, signs on the shelves, adverts in magazines...the works. Brands are almost snookered – they are forced to spend money to maintain exposure, but are failing to achieve the cut-through to consumers they need.

I wish I could help. There must be a better way for my brand and I to attract our customers' attention than shouting at them, interrupting their favourite TV or radio shows with an advert. Surely the customers then just switch off. Isn't there something called 'ad-blocking' where consumers can download apps that block out ads?

Can't we find a medium that manages to get our consumers' attention while remaining affordable?

CAN WE FIND MEDIA TO GET CONSUMERS' ATTENTION WHILE REMAINING AFFORDABLE?

The real challenge is to find media that permits ongoing relationships with our consumers.

In January 2016, circa 20% of the UK adult population used ad-blocking. Predictions then indicated that by January 2017 up to 30% of the UK population would be using ad-blocking. Consumers are more and more in control of the media messaging they encounter. Therefore, our packaging value as a medium can only go up because of its non-intrusive nature.

5. Retail landscape

The retail landscape is changing rapidly. Traditional shops are struggling to retain the attention of consumers when they are in store. Consumers seem to come in and go through whilst on their smartphone. They miss shop media that used to catch their attention. Seem to have their mind on other things. Conventional shopper marketing agencies complain that their messaging techniques can no longer cut through. They're now talking about trying to get into the mind of the consumer before they enter the shop.

If Packaging Could Talk

Conventional retail channels are increasingly being challenged by online retailers. Amazon's entry into the grocery market is an indication of this, and the amazing story of Nestlé launching Nespresso directly to the consumer rather than using the conventional retail route to market is an indication of brands wanting to take control. Brands need closer and stronger consumer relationships.

My brand and I need to find ways to build connections and relationships with our consumers fast, regardless of where they buy us.

6. Consumer engagement

Consumer engagement seems to take central stage in most brand building forums. How can we develop a relationship with our consumers? Interesting question.

The Brand Market Through The Eyes Of A Pack

Because many consumers spend a lot of time on their smartphones and other devices, they often seem to develop genuine relationships with brands that they buy on the internet. I've heard amazing stories of consumers becoming brand ambassadors and sharing a load of stuff with their friends and followers.

Look at the brand Graze that has emerged from consumers subscribing online to a monthly snacking service. The brand knows who its consumers are as they have registered online to a subscription service. This can develop a two-way relationship; the brand can simply ask its consumers questions by sending them an email.

It's not so easy for the brands in traditional retail stores. We have to second guess what consumers are thinking; we can't ask them, and so they often just walk away. It's so frustrating. If only we could have a conversation.

So, it's not easy out there. The media market is cluttered and becoming more and more fragmented; the retail world is changing; and the path to purchase is full of competing communication that makes it difficult to attract consumers' attention. Brands have to seriously consider reinventing their model.

Some FMCG brands have led the way in disrupting their models and reinventing themselves. If Nescafé can upgrade from a jar of instant coffee to a premium designer coffee experience delivered direct to the end consumer, what will ice cream be one day? Freshly delivered to your door with different toppings? What about pizza? Will all pizza brands have to deliver hot pizzas from an authentic wood-fired oven?

What can packaging do to help? Packaging is something every brand has, but it cannot afford to be complacent. It must reframe and reinvent itself to contribute as much as it can to help its brand compete in the marketplace.

The Brand Market Through The Eyes Of A Pack

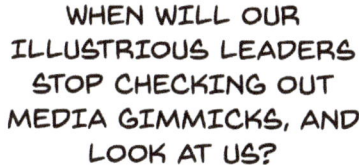

As consumers continue to become smarter and more aware of the products they buy, packaging will continue to play a larger role in brand differentiation through a combination of creative design and embedding new technologies that turn packaging into a lifestyle.

Ryan Campbell
PepsiCo US

The next chapter looks at packaging, its features and how it can be used to help brands grow.

Chapter 2

PACKAGING'S DAY JOB

Before we can seek out the extra value we, as your packs, can bring you, it's important to understand what our main jobs are.

Hold and protect the product

We go through quite a journey! First the product is put into us. Then we are often put into an outer pack to protect us before being loaded into an outer container then on to a pallet.

There was a time when we were simply transported in a lorry to the local shop. But now we are often shipped in containers by air or sea all over the world. God knows where we will end up!

Making sure we are made out of material that is strong enough to take the beating we get in shipment and still look good when we are put on show in the shops is not an easy task.

Advertise the brand

Our brand needs to have a strong identity. A lot of money is spent on making sure that the name of the brand we represent is displayed clearly and the brand message makes a strong statement. A lot of professional designers comment on the designs we use to advertise the brand. Graphical design with print techniques are the key tools we use here.

Some fantastic print effects are possible these days, and an incredible amount of money is spent on new developments. Printing presses, once limited to four colours, now regularly contain eight or even ten colours inline. Printers can give us special effects with the clever use of varnishes, holographic foil blocking or metallic foils. New printing technology also means that we can be made out of metallic foil substrate and still carry print on top. We often look quite posh.

Describe the product

There's so much information that has to be printed on us. What is our product? What is it called? How is it best used? What is our product made of? Addresses, websites, phone numbers, call centre contacts in case of issues... the list goes on.

Often companies have to use really small print to cram in all the information they need to present. Furthermore, a lot of us are sold across many different countries, so this information needs to be translated into several languages. Sometimes you can't even tell where we were originally made.

Make an impact

While being able to hold the product, strong enough to withstand shipping, and covered with necessary information, we still have to stand out on the shelf. We must be shaped and designed in a way that will differentiate us from the competition.

As the saying goes, 'Appearance is everything'. The image we present to our consumers is massively important. Every time a consumer looks at us, from the shelf to the basket to the table, we have a chance to make a lasting impression.

It's easy to put packaging into a box, if you'll pardon the pun. Packaging has traditionally been seen as a cost centre rather than a tool to help add value. We need to constantly reframe how we look at packaging if we want to liberate more value from it.

It comes as no surprise that packaging is an enormous global market, estimated to be worth circa $900 billion per annum, and growing year on year. Let's look at some of the key aspects of packaging with examples of how each packaging feature has been used to the brand's benefit.

Packaging construction

Clearly there are a number of different materials, packaging types and shapes that one can use to pack a product. Shape and construction help a pack to stand out among competitors and can be a very strong enticement for the consumer to purchase. In my career, I have come across many examples of innovative pack shapes. Here are a few of them.

The Smarties tube is an iconic packaging shape that drove the success of the brand. Arguably, the brand should never have stopped selling the product in tubes as the two became synonymous.

Early in my packaging career, I joined a company called Robinson Packaging that developed the packaging technology, spiral wound tubes, for Nestlé Rowntree's Smarties. We used to make and deliver 120 million Smartie tubes a year. In a museum chronicling the company's history, Nestlé cites the decision to manufacture Smarties tubes in-house and stop buying them from Robinson as a major event in their history.

This made massive economic sense to Nestlé as convoluted technology was much less costly than manufacturing and shipping rigid spiral wound tubes.

Smarties tubes are a great example of how shape can develop a relationship with the consumer. The minute I wrote the words 'Smarties tube', I had immediate flashback to putting the tube up to my mouth to pour a Smartie in, then using the tube as a cap cannon after the Smarties were finished. Hitting the base of the tube to fire the cap out was a great game.

Since the launch of Smartie tubes, this format has been more widely introduced for confectionary packaging. In the UK especially, we are used to purchasing confectionary products in round packaging, creating a distinct relationship and association between the two.

Pringles – crisps in a can. Being in the business of spiral wound packaging in my early career, I always remember a conversation with a Swiss machinery manufacturer, Grabher Indosa. The leader in the business of composite round can packaging, Indosa was a specialist in the manufacture of cans typically used for food products like drinking chocolate and sauce granules.

The company had received an enquiry for the manufacture of fifty machines to make over 100 million packages for crisps per annum. Werner Grabher, Indosa's Founder, was used to crisps being packaged in a low cost flexible pack and could not imagine how a pack of crisps could justify the cost of a spiral wound round composite can. He quietly declined the opportunity to quote and scope out the machinery enquiry, thinking that it was a waste of time.

To his astonishment, Grabher learnt a year later that the client had purchased the machines from a competitor for the manufacture of the Pringle can. The round can is an incredible example of how shape can help a brand speak itself off the shelf. Despite the high price, its stand-out appeal in store and the feeling the cans have in people's hands have had a huge influence on the success of the brand. Who would have thought that one could commercially market crisps in cans that cost over 10p each?

Tear and share. A more recent impressive pack construction is a product launched by PepsiCo Walkers called 'tear and share'. Knowing that crisps are often shared over a drink, the company designed the pack to convert itself into a bowl when torn apart. A clever, flexible packaging system, it easily communicates the association between sharing and this brand. This is an example of developing a brand-consumer relationship promoted by the packaging.

TEAR AND SHARE

If Packaging Could Talk

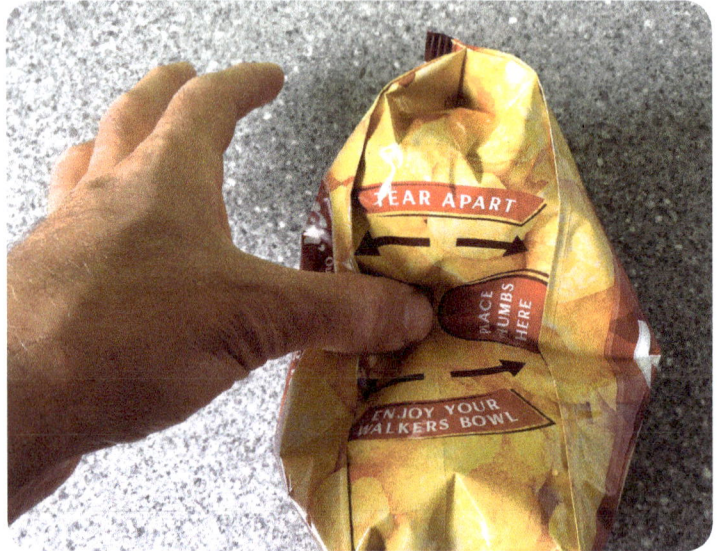

Packaging's Day Job

The flexible stand-up pouch is another good example of a packaging construction that has had a strong impact and helped create a product identity. Serving individual portions of cat food from an upright container became central to the appeal of the product. As such, the stand-up flexible pouch became fundamental to the product's value.

Similarly designed pouches for confectionery have been able to align with the "sharing" concept. A pack of chocolates that can be shared has more value than single consumption, hence the packaging construction has added value through its shape.

STAND UP POUCH

Glass pots. A company that successfully created a £multi-million brand in ambient desserts in fewer than five years is Gü Puds. Recognising a gap in the market, Gü Puds' Founder James Averdieck developed some seriously tasty chocolate puddings.

In a market that was dominated by own brand puddings, it was essential for Gü Puds to differentiate its product and brand. James's decision to focus on unique packaging materials and shapes was a strong contributor to the brand's success. Though little chocolate puddings were being made by several food brands, none were so elegantly served in glass ramekins. These immediately gave the puddings a weight and value which made them special.

A consumer eating the Gü Pud developed an association with the product, largely thanks to the glass ramekin and classy packaging design.

GÜ PUDS GLASS RAMEKINS

If Packaging Could Talk

Yeo Valley yoghurt pots. Yeo Valley, a dairy yoghurt brand, is an example of using an interesting construction to create a stronger connection with the consumer. The yoghurt pot consists of a plastic pot with a printed cardboard jacket glued down a vertical seam. Because the glue is a vertical line, the jacket can be freed when it's torn along a perforation.

By incorporating a zip style mechanism, the cardboard jacket draws the consumer to tear it off and reveal the print on the inside. By making the message something the consumer has to reveal while incorporating an enticement in the construction, Yeo Valley encourages the consumer to participate more with the pack.

SIDE OF YOGHURT TUB

Packaging's Day Job

TEARING THE PRINTED JACKET TO REVEAL MORE

45

If Packaging Could Talk

INSIDE OF THE JACKET

POT SEAL MEMBRANE, OUTSIDE

Packaging's Day Job

SEAL INSIDE REVERSE

Using packaging construction to create an identity. Marks & Spencer's journey into the fresh soup category is an interesting story of a brand using packaging construction to establish an identity and differentiate itself.

Fresh soup was pioneered by a company called The Covent Garden Soup Company. Launching a range of fresh soups that were sold chilled, Covent Garden Soup decided to use Tetra Pak, a unique board pack originally developed for packaging milk. It was very successful, but it wasn't long before supermarket own-brands like M&S and Waitrose began to offer fresh soup ranges.

Interestingly, M&S decided to use a rigid plastic conical pack, like a big transparent cup with a lid on. This was not only a different shape, but it also meant consumers could see the soup. The range gathered momentum, and soon the other supermarkets were copying M&S and launching their fresh soups in similar packs.

How could M&S differentiate further? It invested in a new shape: an oval pack that fitted better in the hand. The latest development has been to improve its oval pack to be shaped like a wave on the face and reverse.

This is yet another great example of using shape to connect with the consumer. On the shelf, there is very little difference between the new shape and the previous oval pack. However, once you pick it up and put it in the microwave, it becomes obvious. The new shape is much easier to handle and hold.

CONICAL SEE-THROUGH PLASTIC PACK

If Packaging Could Talk

OVAL PLASTIC PACK

Packaging's Day Job

OVAL PLASTIC PACK WITH DIMPLES MAKES IT EASIER TO HANDLE WITH ONE HAND

The construction, shape of the pack, and associated product value are all extremely important contributors to developing a relationship with your consumer. However powerful digital communication tools become, the physical shape, design and material of the pack will always play an important role. There are several examples of brands which have underestimated the importance of their packaging and, in an attempt to reduce money, have altered the shape. The Smarties tube is one example of this. Changing the pack was a decision that Nestlé suffered heavily from.

The roles of packaging's construction have, with the odd exception, been to protect the product, transport it to the shops and make it stand out as much as possible on the shelf. There are lots of methods to expand and innovate this role. A box can effectively be made to look like a book. Labels can entice you to read their reverse side or contain mini booklets.

The more elaborate the packaging construction, the higher the cost, and this has been to a large extent the reason why, in grocery FMCG items, it has not generally been as extravagant as it could be. However, there are some great packaging designers, and if brands allocate enough latitude to their packaging budget, they can add significant value to their packs.

Packaging's Day Job

IS IT COST, OR MORE THE ADDED VALUE THAT COMES OUT OF A MORE ELABORATE PACK, THAT BRANDS SHOULD FOCUS ON?

BORING... GIVE ME SOME MORE ELABORATE CONSTRUCTIONS AND I AM CONVINCED I COULD GET THE CONSUMER TO LOOK AT ME IN A COMPLETELY DIFFERENT LIGHT.

Packaging design and print

Packaging design and print effects are understandably huge areas for brands and play an important part in the process of making an impression. What people see is very important, so the visual impact of the pack is often the first step to building a lasting relationship.

Are brands using their designs to attract attention and stimulate a purchase? They do, as I'm sure you can imagine, focus and spend a great deal on packaging design. Coming up with a graphic identity that reflects the brand and attracts purchase is vital. Good designs stand out a mile.

Two designs worth mentioning are:

Gü Puds. I've already mentioned this brand's excellent construction, and it's no surprise that its attention to detail on graphics is also impressive. The black packaging is extraordinary and makes a huge impact on the success of the brand. Consumers are quick to respond to any pack messages Gü ran, a success generated from the clear and fabulous image the pack design created. No wonder that Gü went from zero to being worth £30 million after just five years.

Packaging's Day Job

GÜ PUDS PACKS

55

Kettle Chips use a superb range of packaging designs. By cleverly printing on metallic film, the brand has dulled out the metallic effect across most of the pack, meaning that where it is used, it has a strong impact. The contrast of the matt and metallic gold is surprisingly powerful. However, to print matt black on gold metallic film, the printer has to print several hits of white and then black to dull out the metallic film, making this an expensive option.

KETTLE CHIPS

Packaging texture

Shape and print is one thing, but there is also the whole world of touch. It's arguably an area that has not been used as much as possible. Touch a wooden cheese Camembert box and you know it's not cheddar. The cold, shiny brushed metal bottle of a carbonated soft drink is quite unique.

New digital technology in cutting and creasing board packaging has enabled more ornate cutting, meaning packaging can have a tiered rather than flat feel. The more developments there are in this area, the more packaging can exploit its ability to connect using touch.

Packaging suppliers are developing into more and more radical innovations. Examples include a pack that can show video or has inbuilt music. All such ideas share the same basic aims: to add extra impact on the shelf and encourage consumers to pick up the product.

To date, though, most packaging uses print, shape and touch. These media have their limitations:

- They cannot change their message depending on who is reading it
- Usually print, with no video or sound
- Cannot handle two-way communication

Packaging innovation: four common challenges

The packaging supply industry has a bank of exciting ways to add value, innovate, excite and develop, so it is surprising how few of these ways are actually adopted. Here are four common challenges that packaging developers usually face when trying to improve/add value to their packaging.

1. Cost. The bane of any packaging developer's life is how easily brands focus packaging around cost and cost alone. Because brands see packaging as a cost centre, they don't recognise its true value. The true value of the packaging is difficult to assess or measure, and usually a company has many stakeholders who concentrate on whatever they can see value in. Packaging suppliers are constantly trying to release themselves from this trap.

Why can't we assess packaging as a cost versus value equation with clear measurable logic? Packaging needs to be assessed on the value it contributes towards the brand and the cost assessed against this clear value

Brands have few methods to measure the value of what they buy according to what they value internally. The adage goes that a marketing team knows 50% of its spending is not working, but doesn't know which 50%. Marketing needs better ways to align its spending with a return on investment. There is a host of traditional and new media choices to fit each specific challenge.

Choices from TV, radio or publication advertising; posters, door dropping leaflets and in-store media; digital media, signage, outdoor media, experiential media... One gets approached to spend advertising budgets on a host of different media. Even advertising on a sign in a toilet has developed into a bona fide medium. Choices are multiplying but clarity on where the return comes from is getting to be more and more of a challenge.

Brands need help to choose the right media and extract the most value from it. Often, they don't have enough budget to buy the media they would ideally want and hence are constantly losing ground. Media agencies offer services to advise on media budget usage and buy the media on behalf of a brand at a competitive rate. In truth, brands don't get a true picture of their potential return from advertising choices. The only real way they can develop some science behind their choices is in learning through trial and post campaign measurement.

Packaging can extract additional value from media campaigns, acting as a valuable medium itself. There are limited specialists who can help to show brands how to use packaging as media in its own right. Several advisors suggest that there is media value but few can show a clear road map for a brand to use their packaging as a medium.

The first step for the brand is to actually define what value it apportions to media. This may sound obvious, but brands have not got a simple formula when buying and valuing media. A brand finds it easy to value a product ingredient, specify it and benchmark it

Brands need to put a handle on the value of their media output, then challenge packaging to deliver an equivalent or better value than they get from other media options.

2. Unqualified professional judgement. People developing a new pack often neglect to ask the professionals to assess a requirement, making their own 'unqualified' assessments of the implications of a packaging design.

Some common misconceptions are:

'By increasing the number of colours, you increase the cost'. Very often this is not the case. It depends on the number of colours being used and how available they are to use in the printing process.

'Increasing the amount of board on a pack is really expensive'. Again, this is often false. A lot more board can actually have a very small influence on the price depending on the sheet size going through the press. If one wants to add more board on a pack and the printing sheet is working on a set number of packs per sheet size, quite frequently the sheet size used in not the maximum sheet size the printing press can accommodate. Hence, although there is an increase in board size, the printing costs and converting costs remain the same and the incremental cost for more board is not high. Very often factors of printing and converting are the bulk of the cost.

For these reasons, brand leaders need to give the technical packaging experts and suppliers the challenges and not make unqualified assessments and conclusions.

3. Operational complexity. This old chestnut comes up regularly: 'We manufacture large volumes and need to keep our operation simple' or 'Any change will be difficult'. I call this the 'imaginary dragon in the room'.

Typically, people who have no experience or qualifications still have opinions. Without understanding manufacturing and the supply chain any change is interpreted as complex. Therefore, anything that warrants change is immediately dismissed.

Ironically, manufacturing and supply chain professionals are extremely capable of making changes in their operations efficiently. Many embrace change so long as it is implemented in a professional manner. From my experience, when brands have a focussed, qualified commitment to innovate and improve packaging, it is usually much less complex and time-consuming than they may have originally believed.

4. Thinking outside the box. Many brands think of packaging within narrow constraints. This is a self-limiting psychology. They need to look at packaging as a powerful tool that can help address key challenges such as 'We are finding it increasingly difficult to win our consumers' attention. Any ideas how packaging can help?' or 'Our retailers are eroding our margin and keep reducing the price we can sustainably sell our products for. Any ideas how packaging can help?'

Too often, packaging is restricted to its primary job of packing and protecting a product. But has packaging got more to offer? Is there an additional value to packaging? How can it work harder for its brand?

Packaging has a significant media value when brands give it an independent piece of print. The next chapter describes how a company I founded, Packaging Media Ltd, gave packaging specialised mechanical features of extra print suitable for a media message.

> *We even call our packaging secondary packaging. I mean how ridiculous is that!*
>
> **Alan Potts**
> Insight Director, DS Smith

Chapter 3

PACKAGING MEDIA

It was back in 2005 that my wife persuaded me to move our young family to Barcelona for the summer holidays. Having to commute regularly to and from England, I was introduced to the low cost tickets of easyJet. Wondering how the airline could make any money, I looked into the owner Stelios's model and found that he had several revenue streams. By driving large volumes of passengers through certain airports, EasyJet was able to make income from the things passengers spent money on when travelling. Clever lateral thinking.

How could I use this approach in my field: packaging? I needed to find a new business concept that would move me away from the endless commodification spiral. How could I, like easyJet, find a different earning model from a conventional one? Where was the additional value in packaging?

Packaging has to meet a lot of objectives, but what else could it offer? I looked at packaging from a different standpoint: what would it say about itself if it had a voice?

If Packaging Could Talk

These are some of the ideas that started to flow:

WELL, FIRST OF ALL I'M NOT FREE – MY CUSTOMERS BUY ME.

YES, AND CUSTOMERS PICK ME UP – THEY TOUCH ME, FEEL ME, READ ME BEFORE THEY BUY ME, AND AGAIN ONCE I'M BOUGHT.

Packaging Media

THEY TRUST ME. THEY HAVE BEEN BUYING ME FOR A LONG TIME, SO THEY RECOGNISE AND TRUST ME.

THEY LOOK INSIDE ME...THEY LIKE TO GET MY CONTENTS OUT.

If Packaging Could Talk

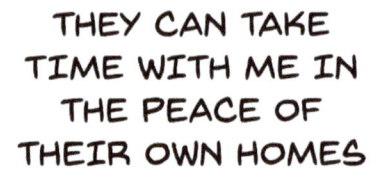

THEY CAN TAKE TIME WITH ME IN THE PEACE OF THEIR OWN HOMES

WE ACTUALLY COMMUNICATE WITH OUR CONSUMERS.

Packaging Media

THEY CAN LEARN A LOT FROM US, LIKE – ABOUT OUR BRAND, ABOUT THE PRODUCT INSIDE US, ABOUT THE RANGE OF PRODUCTS IN OUR FAMILY, AND MORE.

I HAVE SO MUCH SPACE ON ME THAT THERE ARE CHILDREN'S CUT-OUT GAMES PRINTED ON MY BACK!

I realised packaging is a medium, something that consumers read. But here's the dilemma: packaging has a limited amount of space on it. This space has to communicate the brand it represents and all the details of the product inside it. Legal descriptions, instruction for use, contents, etc. – all this makes the space on a pack very precious. It has media value, but the medium is being used for the primary purpose of the packaging which cannot be compromised.

But what if I could develop packaging constructions that allowed the pack to have the same print space and shape, but also included a new feature: an independent piece of print? Surely this would be of value? Could something apparently low in value, like a box of nappy sacks, be transformed into a targeted method to reach mums who have just had a baby? That would be a profitable medium to get those consumers' valuable attention.

I slept on this. Told friends and colleagues about it. Started to show some concepts, and then, in the summer of 2005, decided to commit. I restructured my current packaging company to enable me to spend the majority of my time driving the new business forward, and Packaging Media Ltd was born.

My team and I developed a series of packaging systems with a separate piece of print that the consumer could access without compromising the original shape, construction and print space of the pack. Instead, it would introduce a new media value.

Constructional mechanics

Sleeve media. The first thing we developed involved ready-meal sleeves, a simple method providing a board sleeve with a piece of independent print that consumers could access by tearing a zipper-like tear-off.

Log on to www.turakhia.co.uk to see a dynamic working version of the sleeve media.

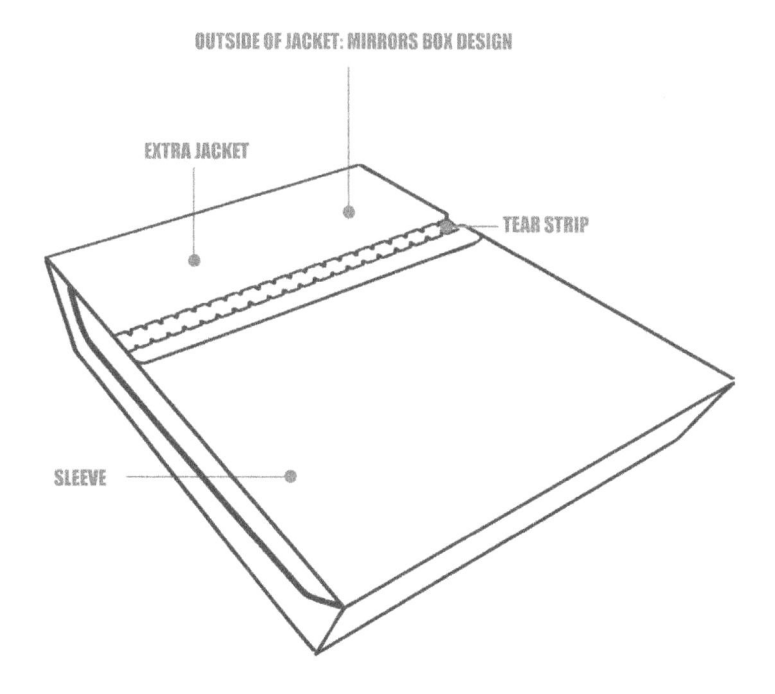

If Packaging Could Talk

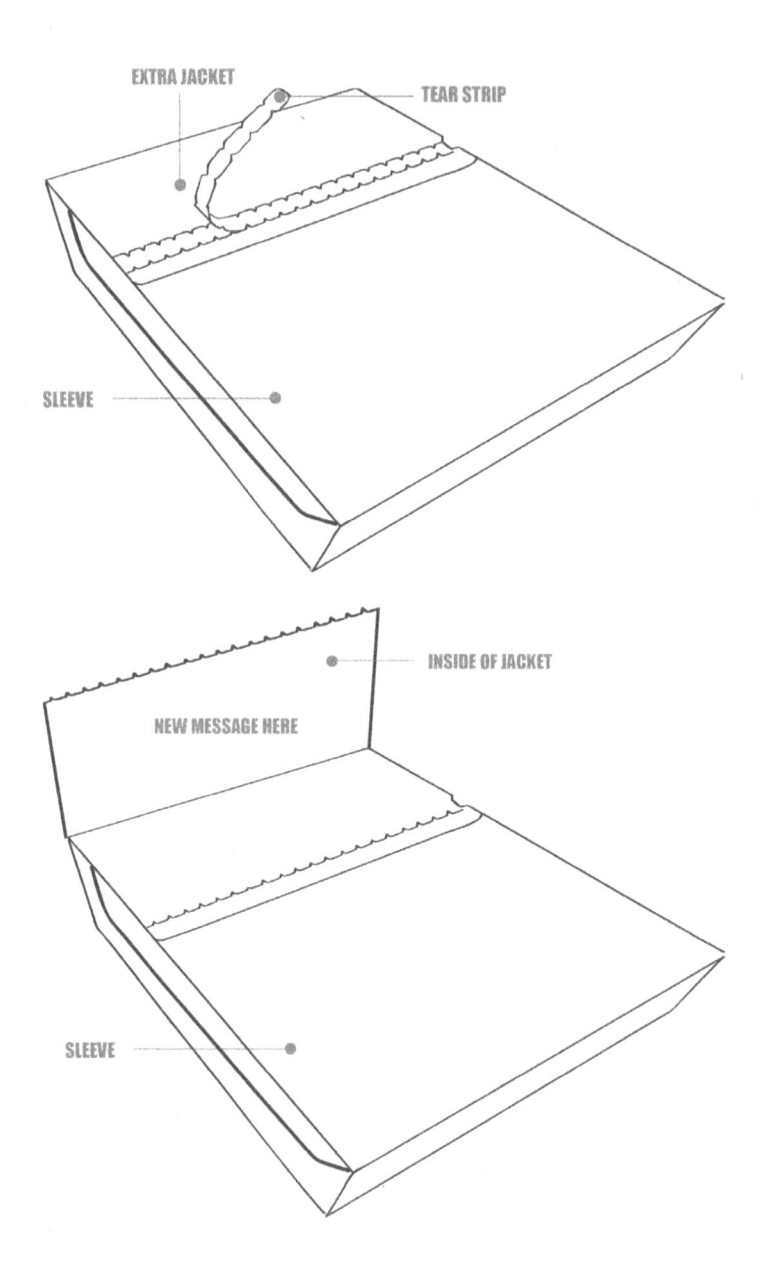

EXTRA JACKET
TEAR STRIP
SLEEVE

INSIDE OF JACKET
NEW MESSAGE HERE
SLEEVE

Box media. The next simple method was to give cartons or boxes an extra jacket with which consumers could again reveal an independent piece of print by tearing a zipper-style tear-off board piece.

Log on to www.turakhia.co.uk to see dynamic working version of box media.

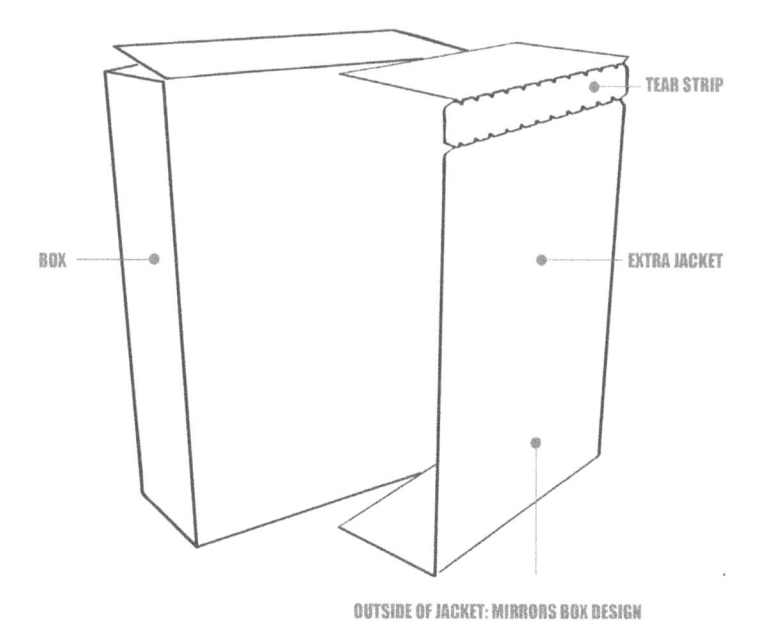

(Diagram labels: BOX, TEAR STRIP, EXTRA JACKET, OUTSIDE OF JACKET: MIRRORS BOX DESIGN)

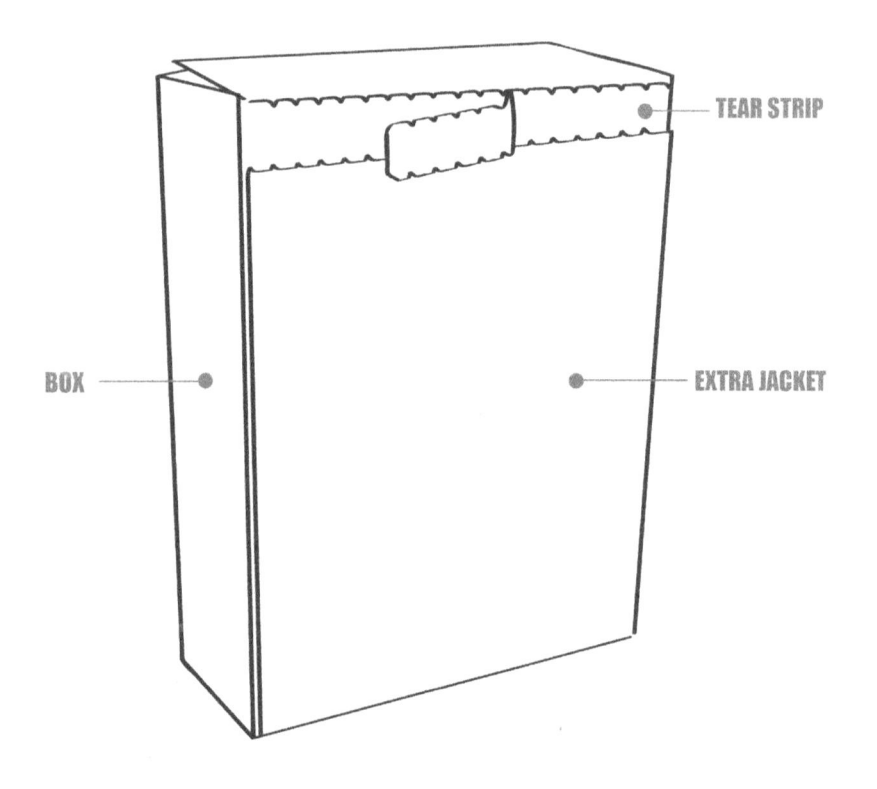

If Packaging Could Talk

BOX

TEAR STRIP

EXTRA JACKET

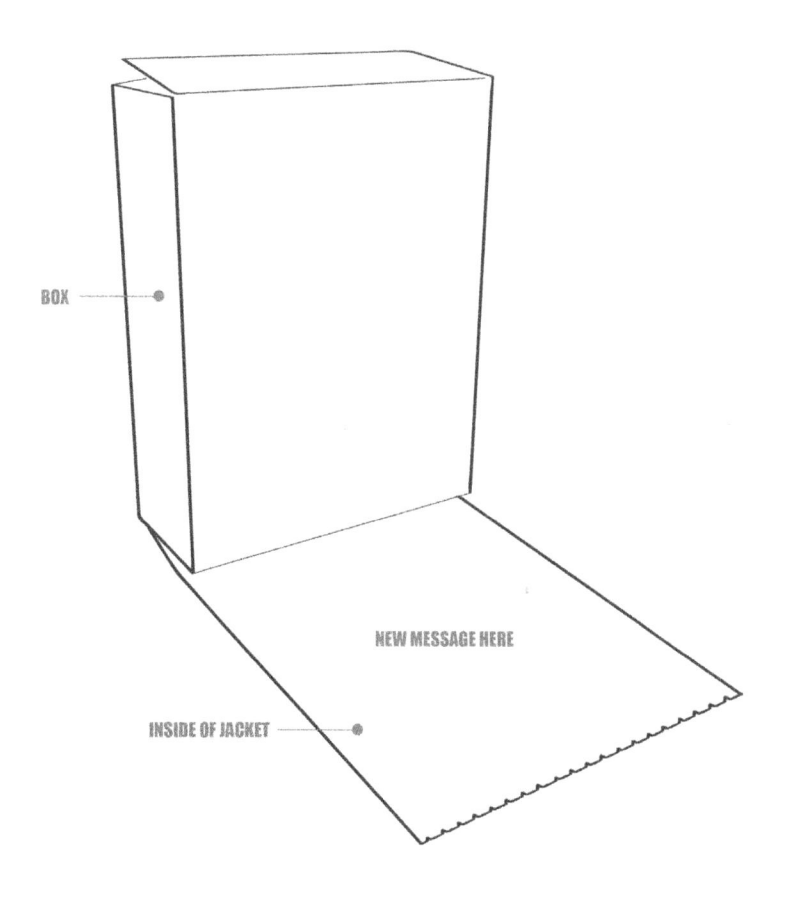

Packaging Media

BOX

NEW MESSAGE HERE

INSIDE OF JACKET

Cup media. Looking at paper cups, I found that those which had secondary walls for heat insulation could be adapted to incorporate a zipper-style tear off, revealing print on the inside of the jacket.

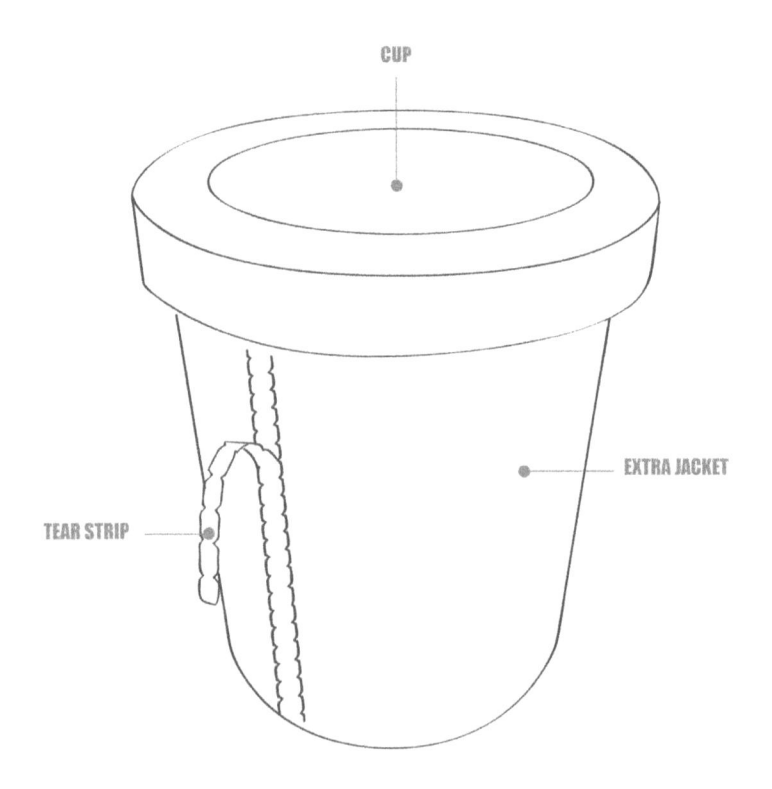

CUP

EXTRA JACKET

TEAR STRIP

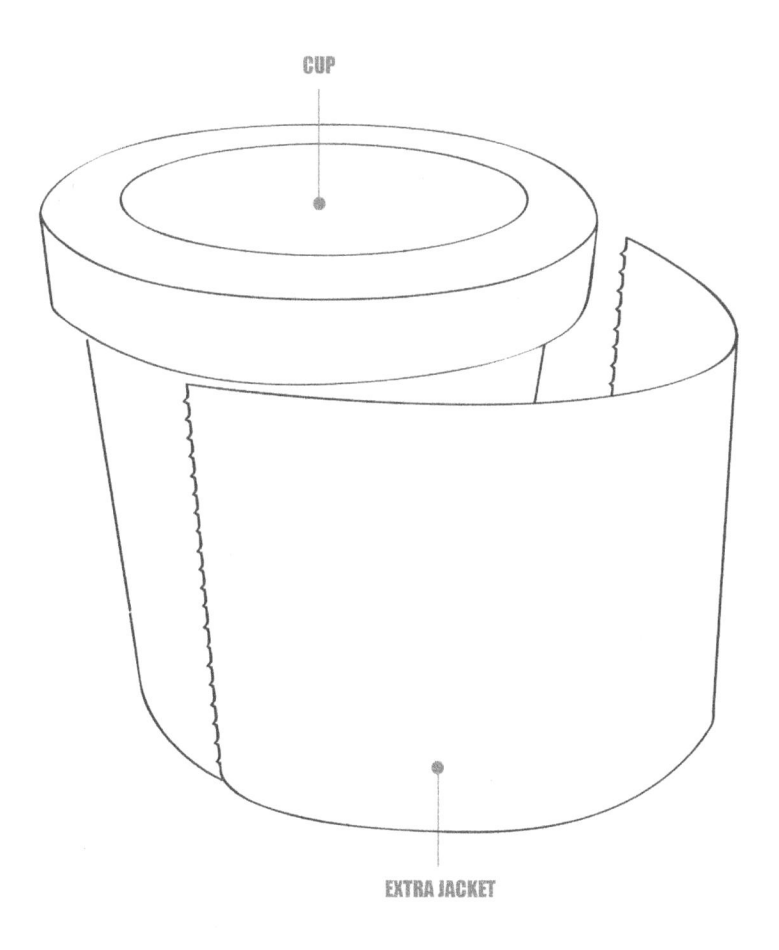

Packaging Media

CUP

EXTRA JACKET

If Packaging Could Talk

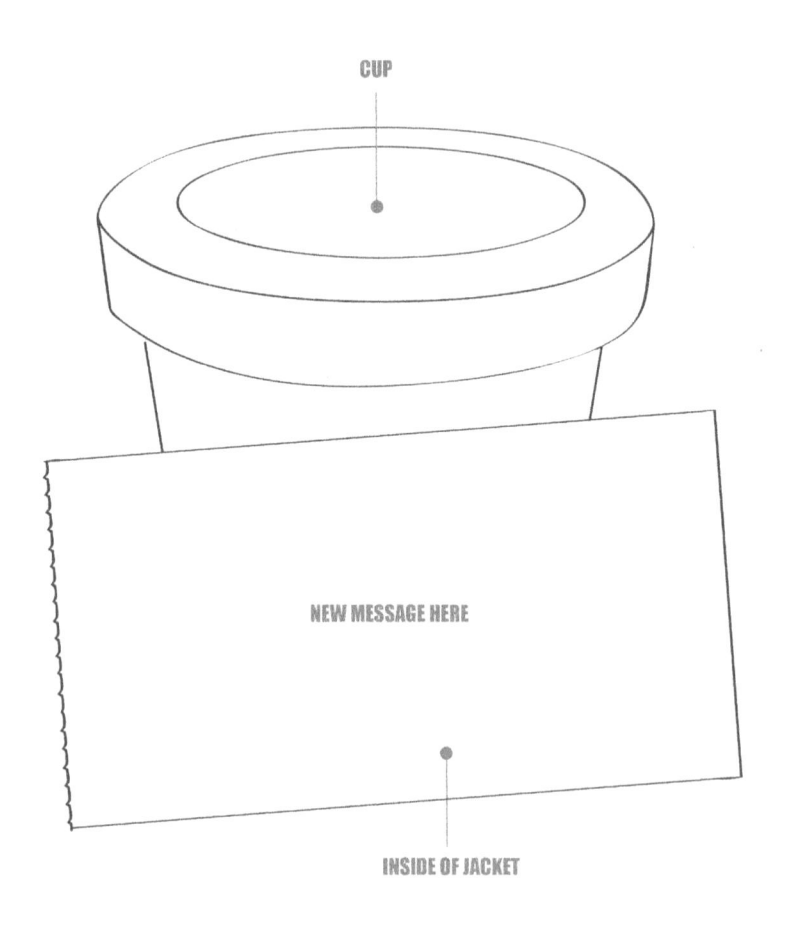

CUP

NEW MESSAGE HERE

INSIDE OF JACKET

You may be familiar with the system McDonald's uses to facilitate its coffee loyalty scheme: buy five and get one free. Consumers collect tokens which can be torn off a section of the coffee cup jacket and stuck on the piece of card. When they have five stickers, they can hand the card over the counter, entitling them to a free cup of coffee.

I was exhibiting my designs at a small packaging show in Birmingham and I had a long conversation describing cup media with a man from McDonald's. He was fascinated about how he could use the inside of the jacket on a coffee cup, and approximately two years later, McDonald's introduced its insulating jacket collector card.

Log on to www.turakhia.co.uk to see dynamic working version of cup media.

Sandwich media. Sandwich packaging had moved into board, and we developed a concept that worked well on sandwich media. Consumers open the cardboard pack to reveal an independent piece of print suitable for communicating another message.

Log on to www.turakhia.co.uk to see dynamic working version of sandwich media.

Mechanics with extra independent space

We gave our systems the Moreinside trademark, the message to the consumer being to tear to reveal more inside. The goal of Moreinside was to develop an enhanced pack that looked the same from the outside as it used to, and brands therefore saw the logic of printing our trademark on their branded packaging.

Using a Moreinside system, we developed packaging mechanics like fix-a-form: booklet labels that provided extra print using concertina designs of folded paper.

We then developed a range of packs that were practical to introduce as packaging options. We knew the costs and saw exciting opportunities to generate a new value for packaging as a medium.

The first step was sign up the medium, i.e. approach brands and ask if they would allow us to use their packs to add additional value to their consumers. We explained that if they used the Moreinside packaging mechanism, we could approach third party promoters and offer them the opportunity to reach more consumers using the independent print. There would be no additional cost for the brand as the third party promoters would typically provide the consumer offer and pay for the costs. They would be, in effect, purchasing targeted media.

Brands would often be worried that the third party offer would not fit their brand positioning. However, the focus of the activity would be to engage the targeted consumers who were already purchasing the brand. Hence, the offer suited the media buyer and the brand.

Consumer gets extra value offer: win.

Brand offers consumer extra value: win.

Promoter reaches their targeted consumer: win.

Our first tasks were to establish the media channel with a range of branded packaging and then take it to agencies operating in the media market. All excited, we approached media agencies on the premise that we had valuable media space that they would want to sell. To our surprise, none of the agencies wanted to help. They thought the idea was clever and confirmed it should carry value, but did not wish to be part of it.

So, we decided we had to sell the media ourselves.

Where is the media value?

Before being able to sell the media, we clearly had to look at the media we had created and understand why we felt it had value. What was it about the packaging that would make it valuable? What justification did we have to ask third-party promoters to pay for the media? How could we sell it?

Rarely do brands scrutinise and focus on the media value of their own packaging. They look at other media and its value at length, but miss the value of their own packaging. The more we looked at packaging, the more evident the value became.

The media value could be justified by segmenting the value in advertisers' terms. Here are the five advertising value areas:

- Consumer audience
- Attention span
- Print
- Brand association
- Lifestyle association

Consumer audience. Media is purchased on the basis of its targeting, and packaging has an exceptional level of targeting. This is not evident at first, but when a pack is compared to other media in its sector, it is a tough act to follow.

Packaged brands can boast a high household penetration in their specific consumer category. Want to reach mums with babies below the age of one? Target nappy sacks. Want to reach mums with toddlers? Try toddler food. Women with children in primary school? Target the type food that goes in a lunchbox. Affluent time-poor singles? Try Waitrose ready meals. White van men? Try pasties or sandwiches. Dog owners? Target dog food. Cat owners? Target cat food. When we looked at sugar, we even found that the size of the sugar bag enabled us to target a specific consumer base.

Attention span. Gaining a consumer's attention is all about being in the right place at the time. Packaging has the advantage that it can communicate at times when the consumer has few distractions and is hence more likely to take notice of the media message. The pack has some media value in the store, but arguably it has much more value after the consumer has purchased the product. At home, the consumer is in an environment where there is much more privacy and much less media competing for their attention.

Packaging commands consumers' attention for a number of different reasons. The pack is used to store the product and the consumer can notice it several times during its use, e.g.

people read what is on cereal boxes while they're eating their breakfast. Oil bottles stay in the kitchen for a long time, and media on the pack can be noticed multiple times. The pack is read to get instructions on how to use the product, e.g. ready meals or pizza boxes. Because the consumer is giving the packaging their valuable attention with few distractions, this is the moment that packaging has its highest media value. If the consumer is enticed to look at a piece of print media at this stage, they are likely to comply.

Print is well known as an effective medium for messaging. Packaging often has large areas of print. What is the print being used for? It communicates three main things:

- Clear brand identity
- What the product is
- How to use it

Lots of extra print, like contact addresses and legal text, also needs to be accommodated. That is a lot of messaging and usually occupies the whole print area.

Sometimes brands try and steal a piece of the print area to communicate a separate promotional message. This works if the pack has a large enough print surface area. For example, cereal boxes manage to carry a promotional message easily. A milk bottle label may find it more difficult.

It's worth noting that two messages can be confusing and compromise the pack's core message, e.g. a promotional message may distract from the core packaging brand message. This usually means that packaging print designs stick to one message and function. Trying to get the print to communicate more than one message is a challenge.

Independent single messaging is clearer and cleaner. Ideally the pack design needs to stay the same but display something that consumers notice, to entice them. Moreinside systems were designed to add an additional independent piece of print for a message without the pack compromising on its main messaging role. The packaging became the carrier for the independent message, which we called being the pack host.

This was the secret of converting packaging into a more effective medium without compromising its core roles.

Brand association. A piece of print that comes unannounced through your letterbox has to communicate its value on its own, and is often quickly discarded. Imagine, instead that the doorbell rings, and someone you respect says, 'Here, I have a piece of print that I recommend you read.'

Packaging media has a well known and trusted brand recommending that the consumer reads a message. A trusted brand telling a consumer to tear endorses the message. Hence the medium has a value simply on account of its message being recommended by the brand. This is the value of brand association. Several examples of this. One to highlight was a promotion we ran with Virgin Vie and online retailer and Cadburys chocolate fingers. We assumed that Virgin Vie would judge the value of their investment on how many direct sales transactions the campaign generated. Actually, the Virgin Vie marketing team and the heads of the business valued the brand association factor of being on a Cadbury's pack that was visible on the shelves for 6 weeks.

Lifestyle association. Media value increases if the message can be given to the consumer in a way that brings the product into context. For example, an advert for running shoes is better placed on the footer of an article by a respected authority on running than on a page about local history or how to brew beer. We called this 'lifestyle association'. If the packaging is holding a product that reinforces the lifestyle theme a third party promoter values, then the media value goes up. A wine brand wanting to associate with 'enjoying a night in', for example, would value the media potential of a pizza box or a large crisp bag, as they are food items people consume when having a night in with friends.

My team at Packaging Media Ltd and I had packaging mechanics that gave packaging an independent media value. We had a sales pitch with which to go to brand packaging owners, the objective being to use their packaging as prospective media hosts. We had a medium able to command the attention of a targeted consumer group using an independent piece of print endorsed by a well known brand and associated to a lifestyle that matched the media buyer's values. Mouth-watering, surely?

Let's find out...

Proving packaging's media value

The first job was to sign up brands willing to let us use their packaging as a medium. The second job was to offer this packaging space to potential promoters who would fill it with offers complementing the brand's product. Simple!

This was new ground, but we had enough belief that we had something of value. So we started selling.

The value of something is only what someone will pay for it. What was the value of our offering? The model was time consuming as there were always two parties to coordinate. However, we successfully managed to show brand owners the value of their packaging. We sold in excess of £500,000 in our first year trading.

One of the first packaging hosts we were introduced to made cake baking kits. A kit typically included shaped trays to bake the cakes, icing, decoration for the cakes, etc. It did not include the cake ingredients.

We were working closely at the time with a company called Ken Wilkins Print, which used to manufacture cake baking kit boxes. An owner of the Wilkins Print and Packaging Group, mentioned the principle of Packaging Media to this client and introduced us. The client was happy to entertain the concept of having a free added-value offer on their pack if we paid for the extra costs and sold the medium to a like-minded promoter.

Cake baking kit boxes: 'what are those?' you may ask. Well, a cheap product to help Mums bake cakes with their children. A kit typically included things like shaped trays to bake the cakes, icing, decoration for the cake style etc. They did not include the traditional cake ingredients. I remember coming back from the meeting thinking, *Who on earth will want to advertise their company on a cake baking kit box worth £1.89?* No immediate advertisers sprung to mind. Like everything in life, this was not going to be as easy as we'd first thought.

Then I considered what we had.

Consumer audience. When I dived deeper into who actually bought a cake baking kit box, I found out some interesting stats. It was parents with children between the age of five and ten who were willing to spend some time baking a cake with their child. Sounds like, well, every mum. But in reality, this isn't the case, not all mothers have the time or desire to do this.

We therefore had our target audience. But what about scale? What percentage of the UK population were parents buying this brand of cake-baking kits? A staggering 80% of UK parents who baked a cake with their children bought this product. If I was an advertiser wanting to reach parents with children between the age of five and ten, what other media would be so precise and targeted? It rapidly became evident that it would be difficult to find a medium that could match the strength of this one.

These cake boxes were:

- Strong in percentage reach of a target consumer group in the UK
- Strong in knowledge of the type of parent its media is reaching
- Strong in the ability to get the consumer's attention because of the time the consumer spends using it

Attention span. The box media system Moreinside provided a large piece of independent print for the mum and child to tear and reveal. A cake takes at least thirty minutes to bake in the oven, so the box could command a lot of the mum's time and attention. Ample for her to reveal the message and digest it.

Brand association. A huge brand – Cadbury's – made these cake baking kits. That connection was worth a lot. The consumer inferred that Cadbury's, a trustworthy brand, endorsed the third party media offer, adding a significant brand association value.

Lifestyle association. This value was not obvious at first, but once we identified it, it proved to be the largest value associated with this product. The medium had a captive audience of parents spending quality family time baking a cake with their children. So the media was directly reaching family-minded mums with children between five and ten. If I was a promoter wanting to reach mums with children aged between five and ten, what other media were there? This was a very targeted group of consumers and research showed there was no comparable medium that could reach so many HHs in such a targeted manner. At best, there were magazines with small readership bases of 20,000-30,000, but nowhere near 200,000 mums.

Once the audience was clearly defined, the task was to ask, 'What kind of organisation would value this target audience? What do parents with children this age spend their money on? Toys? Days out? Cinema tickets? Restaurants with activity centres for young children? Family holidays?

Theme parks seemed an obvious target advertiser. I rang the theme park operators full of enthusiasm with my media proposition. However, I was surprised to hear that they usually sell vouchers to FMCG brands and would not pay for the media to go on brands' packs. I explained to them that they would get an independent piece of print, whereas with traditional packs they only got a small piece of print on the box and were competing with the overall messaging on the pack. They still found it difficult to move from being paid for vouchers to paying to go on this medium, though.

I rang the marketing manager of LEGOLAND and explained my targeted media opportunity. He listened with interest and said that he would think about it. I tried to get back in touch and was not able to reach him, so I sold the medium to a holiday company called Haven Holidays.

A few months later, I rang the LEGOLAND company marketing manager to see if he was interested in a future campaign. He told me he had liked my idea of cake baking kits as medium for him, so had worked with a competitor's cake baking kit. This partnership deal had sold £1.4 million worth of LEGOLAND tickets.

I had sold the medium to Haven for £14,000, and LEGOLAND had shown that this medium could actually drive £1.4 million worth of business. My gut instinct had been right. Packaging media has a value.

My next large coup was signing up a buyer for Waitrose. A very professional lady, as are most John Lewis members, was launching a range of ready meals and really liked the idea of our Moreinside mechanic on the packaging sleeves to provide an added value on-pack promotion. So long as we could provide an offer from a promoter that reinforced the healthy product-positioning, she would allow us to use the packaging.

The packaging media value of Waitrose ready meals was mouth-watering: targeted upmarket time-poor professionals. Waitrose prices usually mean the consumer is among the better off, classified as AB in a demographic segmentation. (Approximated Social Grade with its six categories, A, B, C1, C2, D and E, is a socio-economic classification produced by the ONS – UK Office for National Statistics – by applying an algorithm developed by members of the MRS Census & Geodemographics Group.)

A ready meal takes ten minutes to cook, during which time you can communicate to the consumer. Great brand association:

Waitrose/John Lewis gets such strong brand trust. Lifestyle association: a ready meal called 'Perfectly Balanced' immediately targeted health conscious individuals.

Once we started thinking of potential promoters who would find this media of interest, it was quite easy to make a shortlist. David Lloyd Leisure, an upmarket group of gyms with tennis courts and swimming pools, wanted to promote its gym membership and target professional higher earners. A healthy range of ready meals was a perfect medium for it to offer a free two-day pass worth £70.

We ran the promotion with David Lloyd Leisure, and got a sensational response. Over 14,000 people responded and registered for a free pass when they had satisfied themselves that there was a David Lloyd gym close enough to where they lived. The value of a person signing up to a David Lloyd Leisure gym was approximately £1,200 per annum. So, the media value of circa half a million ready meal sleeves delivered 14,000 valuable prospective customers who lived in close proximity to a David Lloyd Leisure gym, worth £16.8 million.

In retrospect, we should have done a deal which took a percentage of the business that resulted from the media campaign. Certainly valuable media.

Having some real life examples of media buyers using packaging, we were able to sign up a brand called Prima Fresco that sold a large range of pizzas in Tesco. Circa one million boxes became available every other month. While the brand was not able to give us an independent piece of print, they were happy for us to have a section of the box on the face and the reverse for £10k per million boxes. In the first year we sold circa £240,000 worth of media on the pizza boxes and generated an additional income of £120,000 for Tesco. More importantly, we added value for the consumer and increased the value a pack delivers for the brand.

Lifestyle association was a main driver in selling to a variety of promoters interested in pizza boxes as a medium. Promoters who suited the theme of 'a night in' – pizza, ice cream, beer, wine etc – all had a lot to gain from the Prima Fresco boxes' media value.

A good example of a brand seeing the 'product association' value was Tabasco Sauce. Tabasco had a US led directive to get consumers to try the sauce with pizza. The opportunity to advertise on pizza boxes resulted in Tabasco spending regular media budgets on Prima Fresco pizza. With regular commitment to the media, Tesco was cashing in over £100k per annum just for allowing a section of their pizza boxes to advertise a brand and provide the consumer an extra offer.

Other campaigns we ran with dynamic models include Tesco Chinese ready meals, where we were able to convert a ready meal sleeve to incorporate two coupons on it – 75p off an EJ Gallo wine and a free DVD rental offer for Screenselect, a new DVD rental company.

The ready meals enjoyed a 5% uplift in the rate of sale; the wine company gained good product association with a night in

Packaging Media

occasion and brand exposure in a aisle shopped by 14 million shoppers every week and a 2% response in coupon redemption, with over 40,000 sales of wine resulting from the campaign.

We executed two campaigns on the packaging of Charlie Bigham's upmarket ready meals (restaurant quality food with fresh ingredients as a ready meal) with Waitrose.com and Haagen Dazs ice cream. We converted their sleeves using sleeve media.

Campaign 1 was 'Win a year's supply of wine with Waitrose.com', with the purpose of adding value to the ready meal and increasing the rate of sale, while for Waitrose.com it was to raise awareness of their wine offering.

Over 2.2% of the sales resulted in a shopper entering the competition and over 15% noticing the promotion.

Campaign 2 was 'Win a year's supply of Haagen Dazs ice cream + claim a money off ice cream coupon'. This promotion ran on a range of summer barbecue products called Sizzlers with the purpose of adding value to the ready meal and increasing the rate of sale; and for Haagen Dazs to promote directly to Waitrose shoppers.

Over 1.2% entered the prize draw and over 1% took up the coupon.

Bigham's is a good example of a brand that has seen the media value of their packaging beyond its traditional use. They have a permanent board flap on their ready meal packaging designed to entice the shopper to read the pack more and build a connection with the brand.

Quorn food products plus a DVD rental company was an odd campaign and worth mentioning. Where is the connection with Quorn, a meat substitute, with a DVD rental company?

Well, this campaign had astonishing results. Promoting a DVD rental service, it generated over 1600 actual trialists of the DVD rental service, over £50,000 of media value for the DVD rental company. If 1600 people responded then the rule of thumb would be at least 10 times this figure wanted to respond and did not get around to it.

So, we had proven that packaging media is a valuable asset. It delivers results. It is non-intrusive – consumers read the message because they want to, and digest it enough to respond if they find the offer of interest. So why weren't brands using their packaging as a medium more? If promoters could extract £millions of value from promoting a message using packaging as a vehicle, surely the brand itself could use its own media to similar effect?

By providing mechanics that allowed packaging to act as a media channel without compromising its obligations, we unlocked a key to value. Waitrose ready meals proved to be worth £16 million to David Lloyd Leisure, while cake baking kits sold over £1million worth of theme park entry tickets. There was, and is, an untapped potential for packaging to provide an independent medium for the brand, a valuable space to help it grow.

Packaging Media can also get consumers to register online and consent to give their email addresses for future correspondence with the brand. Enter the world of data.

We had shown packaging has a physical untapped media value, but was there a possibility for it to have a digital media value? The next chapter takes the story further and talks about our experiences in helping brands extract value from the new digital world.

> *Future packaging should, besides being sustainable, provide more information than meets the eye. Smart technology opens up limitless opportunities.*
>
> **Paul Mak**
> Graphic Quality Manager,
> Heineken International BV

Smart connected packaging can help build brand value. Brand owners innovative enough to take pioneering steps should look at new opportunities within packaging to enhance their brand's value. Connecting packaging to the exciting world of big data using smartphones and the web can extract hidden value within packaging. Packaging can be central to building an active one-to-one relationship between the consumer and the brand. We believe our products at Benders Paper Cups are uniquely placed to leverage these new ways of customer interaction, whilst they enjoy their coffee or tea.

Allan Paterson
Technical and Development Manager,
Benders Paper Cups

Chapter 4

PACKAGING'S DIGITAL MEDIA VALUE

The David Lloyd Leisure campaign on Waitrose Perfectly Balanced ready meals proved the media value of packaging was not just an idea. After the promotion, we understood that David Lloyd Leisure had got 14,000 prospective consumers of real value who lived close to a gym. These people were more than likely in the higher income category and were interested enough to take the time to register their details for a free gym trial.

After the promotion ended, Waitrose sent us the list of consumers who had responded to this promotion, a rich data source. To our astonishment, we discovered neither David Lloyd nor Waitrose were set up to exploit the value from it.

Many brands are not maximising the media value of their packaging. Even more remarkably, they do not have effective systems with which to exploit the value of having data records if their consumers opt in to communication. If the media value of 550,000 Waitrose ready meals amounted to 14,000 consumers interested in David Lloyd, the potential value to David Lloyd was circa £16 million. What would the value be for Waitrose?

Using a life cycle value approach of a Waitrose ready meal consumer and a few assumptions, one could speculate that each consumer would buy two ready meals, valued at £8, a week. That means 14,000 consumers were worth £112,000 per week.

Therefore, these consumers could have been worth £5.8 million per annum to Waitrose.

So the media value for a campaign on 550,000 Waitrose consumers, generating 14,000 consumers, might have been worth circa £16 million to David Lloyd Leisure and £5.8 million to Waitrose.

Brands spend a lot of time trying to win over new customers into their category, so if they can capture the data of individual customers, surely it makes sense to incentivise them to buy the brand frequently.

Until now, brands have not been able to consider a world where they can practically market to individual consumers. The new digital tools of the internet and the cloud and databases open up the opportunity not only to store consumers' data, but to use it to understand them on a new level. On top of having value to promoters, packaging could also get consumers to volunteer their data to the brand.

Packaging Media Ltd, focussing on the media value of packaging, was quickly exposed to the traditional market of on-pack promotions. There were two things that we observed:

1. Brands were not exploiting the value of data
2. Brands which were running an on-pack promotion did not always require the consumer buy the product to participate in the promotion

The law at that time said that if brands wanted to offer extra value to their customer by means of an on-pack promotion, they had to run it as a 'no purchase necessary' promotion. I.e., consumers were entitled to participate in the promotion without having to buy a product. This seemed crazy to us, and fortunately the ruling changed in the UK allowing brands to run 'purchase necessary' promotions.

i.e. Promotions whereby the consumer could be asked to buy a product and prove they had, in order to participate in the promotion were allowed.

We recognised that brands needed an easy method for consumers to prove they had purchased the product. Working with Goodfella's Pizza, we developed a practical system for brands to have a unique alphanumeric code printed on the pack and used by the consumer as a proof of purchase code. Every code had to be differently generated using random logic so that it could not be copied.

The birth of smart connectable packaging

If every pack carried a unique code, could every pack be connected to the digital age?

Up until now, packaging has proven it can be a medium by using print, design and graphics. Powerful. But the new digital world is emerging: a world in which consumers can share music, sound and videos easily. What if packaging could connect to the digital age?

Clearly, for this to happen, packaging needs to be connected to the internet. Giving every pack a unique ID that can be entered on the web and verified as proof of purchase, neatly linked the offline pack with the online digital space.

Every pack could carry a unique code. If a consumer entered the code on the website the code could be verified against a logic and used as a proof of purchase.

Once a unique code has been entered by a consumer, if they try to enter it again, it will not work. This gave us a secure method whereby the consumer could prove that they had purchased the product.

We realised in our company, renamed Hive IP, that we would have to make it easy for brands to print a unique code on their pack. They could already print sequential date codes on their packs, but could not yet print unique codes. Hive IP developed hardware and software to overcome this issue and make it easy for brands to print unique codes using existing inline factory printing machines.

With brands having the ability to print unique codes on packs, Hive IP then had to provide an easy digital web interface on which the consumer could register their details, enter their code to prove they had purchased the product and redeem the reward the brand wished to give them in return for their custom.

Coinks™

To recap, Packaging Media Ltd found that a promotion on a pack could get a consumer to respond. Brands did not have a proof of purchase system to link consumers to a promotion, nor were they collecting the consumer data records for those who responded. Traditional methods, where consumers were asked to post in a receipt and a form with their name and address, did exist, but if systems did not store the consumer data and behaviour, it could not be easily and cost-effectively used again.

The power of websites and digital databases meant that it was possible to build a system that could do just that. The digital infrastructure which Hive developed was called Coinks™. Brands were able to run an on-pack promotion by inviting consumers to register their details on Coinks™ and enter the unique code from their pack to gain access to the consumer reward.

This was all exciting stuff. But there were still several questions to be asked.

1. Would consumers respond to an on-pack promotion, go online and register their details? Was that too much to ask? Brands were thinking consumers needed instant results.

2. Would consumers actually take a unique code from a pack and enter it on a website to enter a prize draw or claim a special offer?

3. Would consumers respond to further correspondence and purchase more of a branded pack to participate in more promotions?

Could we show brands the power of consumer data and the use of codes to prove purchase? We wanted to test the points listed above, and fortunately Goodfella's Pizzas wanted to run a promotion to engage families using two-day passes for family days out. Although Goodfella's did not have a long-term vision to link their promotions to purchase or indeed collect consumer data, this promotion provided us with a great opportunity to see if it was possible to communicate directly to consumers and get them to buy more pizza.

Would consumers register on Coinks™ to enter their codes from a Goodfella's box and claim their family two-day passes? An on-pack message resulted in over 2%, 40,000 consumers, responding to the pizza box, registering their details online and entering codes.

Learning: consumers would respond to on-pack media, transfer their data and enter a unique code if they were interested in the promotion.

Could we get consumers to buy more pizza? With no mention of it on the pack, we posted a prize draw on the website to win a family holiday to a Spanish theme park. We sent an email to the consumers who had registered for their two-day pass, inviting them to participate in the prize draw. The conditions for entering were:

- Consumers had to purchase a Goodfella's pizza and enter a code
- The more codes they entered, the better their chances were to win

By communicating the increased chances, they would have if they entered more codes, we showed consumers how they could influence their chances of winning. Lots of consumers engaged with this fact and entered over 5 codes per consumer. That meant an extra 5 pizza sales each.

We proved to ourselves that consumers would purchase pizzas in order to enter a prize draw and would enter codes from the pack. If they wanted to win, they would buy more pizzas and enter more codes. This was interesting. It was clear to us that brands could use their packaging effectively as a net to catch consumer data. Then, they could link their consumers back to the packaging to participate more closely with branded promotional activity. Powerful stuff.

Although brands were not necessarily looking to develop large databases of consumers to promote directly to, Coinks™ helped them to run their promotions. By default, Coinks™ itself obtained a consumer database of over two million households that had registered from a branded on-pack promotion that needed them to enter a code. Consumers would register on Coinks™ and earn points from entering codes from participating branded packs. Points could be exchanged for free products, entries into prize draws, and exclusive money-off vouchers.

Consumers participated if offered something of interest, and would take the time to register online and enter a unique code from a pack. A two-way relationship between a consumer and a brand was then born.

Typically, grocery brands had always dealt with a large wholesale distributor, who would in turn sell to a retailer. Retailers would have the direct contact with the end consumer. Brands did broadcast advertising to their consumers, but did not recognise the value of having individual direct conversations with them. Existing data systems would not be able to handle this contact. But with the cloud's ability to cope with large amounts of data, brands are now in a position to communicate directly to consumers, learn more about them and promote directly to them.

How far a consumer will go if they want something badly enough can be best illustrated by the story of a lady who bought bleach. Early on in Hive, we ran a promotion on a bleach brand called Easy. It was a simple campaign: 'Win a kitchen worth £2,000. Buy a bottle of Easy bleach, and enter the unique code from the pack to participate.'

But it was not *that* simple. There are two problems with prize draws: consumers never think they are going to win, and consumers have no chance to influence whether they win. It's very much pot luck.

Maybe our unique code prize draws could address these issues. When the consumer entered their code from the bleach bottles, we could tell them their odds of winning and how they could improve those odds: simply go and buy another pack and enter another code. The more packs they buy, the more codes they can enter and the better chance they will have of winning the kitchen.

The results were amazing. Even though most households need a maximum of two bottles of bleach per week, many consumers entered several codes to maximise their chances to win. When we did the draw, we found the lady who won had entered over 200 codes. Surely she had not bought 200 bottles? Was this a fraudulent shopkeeper or a warehouse employee stealing codes?

We sent a polite note to the lady asking her whether she had any proof she could provide us of purchasing 200 bottles of bleach. To our astonishment, she had already entered unique codes indicating she had purchased the products. To prove she had not stolen the codes without purchasing, she sent us pictures of cupboards full of bleach. She lived in an army complex and had asked all her friends to buy this particular brand of bleach and give her the bottle. She and her friends must have spent £200 on bleach to give her a chance to win a £2,000 kitchen. Fortunately, she won!

Learning: consumers will purchase more and enter codes to do something they are engaged with. This lady wanted a new kitchen and liked prize draws. She particularly liked prize draws where she could influence her chances of winning.

The lesson in 'seeds'

Coinks™ gave consumers the choice of how to use their points. But an early lesson was that brand managers or marketing managers had to understand their consumers well enough to know what they valued.

Coinks™ had a host of different rewards for consumers to spend their points on and it was always interesting to see which were the most popular. It was most often the ones that no one would have guessed.

Many readers over forty may remember Blue Nun wine. Blue Nun was a successful German wine sold in the UK, and students bought lots of it as it was attractively priced. But over the years, Blue Nun has lost market share and publicity to a wide selection of wines from all over the world.

Around 2008, the company approached us and wanted us to see if we could drive our Coinks™ consumer database to

Packaging's Digital Media Value

persuade consumers to buy Blue Nun wine. What a test! I asked everyone I knew if they would buy Blue Nun wine, and the typical answers were, 'Well, I used to buy a lot in my student days, but can't remember when I last bought one' or 'That sweet stuff we used to drink when we were students? I didn't know it was still available.'

I put the challenge to Nick Evans, our specialist in data and consumer engagement. Nick said he could profile the Coinks™ consumer database – consumers who had responded to a promotion – and offer them something relevant to entice them to go and buy a bottle of Blue Nun wine.

This wasn't an easy task. Coinks™ consumers were consumers who had responded to a promotion. (i.e. they had to enter a code from a branded pack to participate in the promotion.)

Nick would have to:

- Segment the Coinks™ database
- Send consumers an email offering them something he thought would engage them as a reward for buying a bottle of Blue Nun wine
- Hope that they'd enter the code from the bottle online and redeem their offer

The first job was to print a unique code on every bottle of Blue Nun wine. We did this using Hive IP's practical code printing system and installed it on the wine bottling line. Every bottle of wine carried a unique code with no reference to it on the bottle, and no messaging on the bottle. All the messaging would have to come from digital media.

Blue Nun was stocked in Asda, but did not get much shelf space. The plan was to send Coinks™ consumers an email offering them 100 Asda reward points, a value of circa £1, if they purchased a bottle of Blue Nun (then priced at circa £4.50) from Asda, came back to the Coinks™ website and entered the code. Before they could even buy it, the consumer had to find the bottle of wine, usually on the bottom shelf – altogether not a simple task.

I was astonished to read the results. A targeted email campaign to circa 200,000 consumers on Coinks™ delivered a retailer sales uplift of 4.65%, which was the equivalent of the ongoing weekly sales of ten Asda stores. On top of that, 48% of the consumers who responded hadn't bought Blue Nun prior to the promotion, 79% purchased more Blue Nun as a result, and 68% would continue to buy Blue Nun after the promotion.

Learning: if we could get consumers to go into a store, find a bottle of wine, buy it, come back and enter a code, then it was clear that there was value in data. With the relevant reward, they were happy to buy a product and prove they had purchased it by entering a code.

Our results were starting to get interesting. We had proven that consumers would enter a code from an on-pack promotion several times. We were learning about relevance and how we can't second guess consumers. It is all about providing them with something that is relevant to them, and what engages them is very often a surprise.

Our promotion for Tetley tea, involving the newly launched Green tea, was a fantastic example of incentivising consumers using relevance. Tetley wanted consumers to try its new product so decided to run a 'Try me free' promotion on its packaging.

'Try me free' is a standard type of promotion that brands use to drive trial. The consumer buys the product, proves they have purchased it and receives their money back. Traditional methods would involve the consumer having to send their receipt proving purchase to a company address along with a self-addressed stamped envelope to receive their cash refund. Cumbersome.

With our unique code proof of purchase system, we were able to ask the consumer to register on a website and enter the unique code to prove they had purchased the product. They could then claim their refund online.

As a test to understand consumers better, we decided to try an alternative offer. All the consumers responding to the promotion were coming for a cash refund. There was no other reason for them to be participating in the promotion. So, when they entered their code and proved they had purchased the product, we decided to give them two options: a cash credit by BACS for the full £1.79 cost of the tea or an option to donate that money to plant one metre squared of rainforest.

What percentage of consumers who had come online to get their money back do you think opted for the rainforest distraction offer? It was 40%.

Ironically the brand had to pay a lot less than the cash refund to plant one metre squared of rain forest. Tetley saved money and learnt what its price sensitive customers valued. Tetley got endorsement that their brand desire to be environmentally friendly resonated with their consumers - even the price conscious ones.

Learning: engagement does not have to be more expensive. By knowing what a consumer wants, you can engage them at a much lower cost than a cash refund. Perceived value can be much higher than cash.

Contrary to naïve preconceptions, we discovered it was not just a few prize-draw geeks who would enter a unique code. In fact, a study of code entry across two million consumers showed that the profile of people who would enter a code pretty much mirrored the profile of the UK consumer base. Brands were now allowed to run purchase necessary promotions, and were realising that consumers would enter codes to participate. Hive IP's pack passport system, which helped brands to print unique codes on packs, was providing brands real value. By providing brands with a simple, thought-through system to help them manage the printing and management of unique codes, we were in demand.

PepsiCo is a brand which typically likes to take promotional decisions one tactical campaign at a time. A big change in the

Packaging's Digital Media Value

market came when PepsiCo decided to take a much more strategic view on proof of purchase and codes. It installed the Hive pack passport system printing solution in its factories for three years to cover its coding requirements, making its coding significantly lower cost and easier to adopt. PepsiCo was able to save a lot of money on its coding, but more importantly, it could run larger unique code promotions, driving more sales and grow its market share. This coincided with PepsiCo having the money to sponsor the high profile UEFA Champions League football competition.

One of the most impressive promotions we have been a part of drove consumers to collect letters to spell the name of a holiday destination and win a free holiday. The United Kingdom has a household population of only circa twenty-seven million. The promotion ran for two months and managed to get a massive twenty million unique codes entered. Over 700,000 consumers participated, and each consumer was so engaged in the promotion that on average they entered thirty codes each. In fact, more than 90,000 consumers entered over 100 codes during the two-month period of the promotion.

Learning: packs are a powerful medium to get consumers to engage. If you can get the right engagement then they will participate. Unique codes, even alphanumeric codes, are easy for a consumer to enter – certainly easier than typing out credit card details.

Billions of codes are distributed and entered every year. Whereas technology providers are trying to push grocery brands to include chips – NFC tags – into their packs, the only ubiquitous solution to make FMCG packs smart is unique codes. Technologies like NFC are very exciting as they eliminate the need for the consumer to enter a code. If the pack has NFC all the consumer has to do is tap the pack. The costs for this are high; however the value packaging is yet to be fully realised. With focus on showing brands the value, we could live in a world where a bag of sugar that costs 50p holds a NFC tag costing 10p, because of the holistic value that technology enables.

Consumers do things only if they want to. Brands need to focus on making their consumers want to participate, either with a code, a NFC tag, or any new technology that facilities consumer participation.

So, the digital age was upon us. Everyone was talking about big data, but there were still very few real examples in the grocery FMCG market of brands using big data and translating it to practical applications that helped them grow.

Packaging pushed through a barrier. It became 'smart' smart because it had a method to connect consumers to the digital world, which had the power to be more relevant, valuable and individual to them. Packaging could certainly attract consumers to respond to a promotion and register online and enter a code. This involved the consumer opting in to provide their data online and start a two-way relationship with the brand.

Consumers like to choose their rewards and will enter lots of codes if brands engage them. Data profiling tools mean brands can store consumer behaviour and get clever with connection. It is possible to drive behaviour.

All the evidence has shown that FMCG brands have a powerful new tool available. The 'internet of packaging', 'smart packaging' or, more specifically, a unique pack ID connects a consumer wanting to opt in for a digital communication with the brand. The cloud and digital database structures make it practical for brands to contemplate hosting data of all their individual consumers and learning about them through direct communication. The unique pack ID provides specific purchase intelligence, eg what product was purchased and when.

Will consumers change their behaviour? Yes, they will act if brands give them a reason to do so. Can the data be used to drive extra sales? Yes, the consumer has to purchase the product before they can participate in a promotion. Hence promotions using unique codes are more likely to increase sales. Furthermore, if a consumer handles and interacts with the branded pack, they are more likely to remember what brand they bought and buy it again. A consumer who has entered thirty codes from branded packs over two months must be familiar with the brand.

A direct connection between a consumer and the branded pack has, arguably, a larger value than indirect media messaging. The true value of this has not been extrapolated back into FMCG accounting terms.

What would a pack say?

'Brands, you tell me you want more sales, stronger relationships with your consumers. You spend loads of time looking at expensive media solutions and sales promotions to try and drive incremental purchase. What about us? Spend a small amount on us and we will show you what powerful media we are!

'We can get our consumers to have real relationships with us. We have a true understanding of what our consumers like. They understand that we, their packs, speak their language. We hold the key.'

Brands are sitting on a mountain of value with their packaging. A powerful, direct medium. Quite simply, packaging is one of the most powerful media tools brands have. On top of this, it's a free medium for the brand.

Brands can use unique pack IDs to encourage consumers to:

- Purchase for the first time
- Purchase more frequently
- Be more loyal
- Develop stronger relationships with the brand
- Recommend the brand to friends and family

There are lots of market case studies where my company, Hive IP, has wrestled with real CPG, (consumer packaged goods) problems and used smart packaging, connected packaging and intelligent promotional tools to help.

Some examples include:

Discovery Foods, a Mexican food brand, wanted to add some extra tangible added value to their product. A coupon off a Mexican beer sounded like a good match. They had two options:

1. Print a coupon on the pack.
2. Use a code and a website to deliver the coupons.

With likely response rates, a 50p coupon on the pack could get 20% valuing the coupon, leading to a sales uplift instore of 5% and perhaps 5% actually using.

Cost would be 2.5p per pack.

Promote a £2 coupon on pack but the consumer has to log on to a website, enter their details and get a unique code to print off a £1 beer coupon.

This would get 40% valuing the offer leading to a 15% sales uplift and perhaps 2.5% actually redeeming the coupon. Cost per pack would be 2.5p per pack.

Discovery Foods ran the latter and got a larger sales uplift than 15% due to the added value offer on the pack.

As an added bonus, Discovery Foods obtained over 40,000 consumer records of their shoppers who valued beer with Mexican food.

Anchor Butter ran a long-term programme where consumers could redeem free gifts and enter enticing prize draws in return for buying packs and entering codes.

Anchor's average frequency of purchase was 4 per household. The programme managed to get the average participant to enter 7.8 codes each, so almost doubling their frequency of purchase. The active members entered 22.45 codes each! Hence, the programme increased them to buy over 5.6 times they normally would.

Clearly some shoppers may have already purchased at this frequency and just received an added gift of thanks for their loyalty. But the number of participants suggested that Anchor successfully increased their frequency of purchase using intelligent coded packaging and a digital website.

Andrex toilet paper wanted to add value to their product offering and ensure brand loyalty, so they ran an on-going campaign called Puppy Points that offered brands points for purchasing packs which carried unique codes on them. Consumers could redeem a host of rewards in return for their points.

Andrex had a successful campaign, and when they measured with Nectar, a Sainsbury's sales data exercise, it proved that members were much more loyal than non-members.

Kellogg wanted to run a sales promotion without reducing the selling price of their cereal from around £3 a box. The retailer wanted them to reduce the price to £2.50. Kellogg needed a promotion that provided the consumer extra value, reason to buy but not reduce the price.

Kellogg ran a unique code short-term collector promotion with a message on the front of the pack: 'Claim a free pack of cereal'; and a message on the back of the pack: '3 packs required'.

The consumer would enter three codes from the pack and be provided with a coupon for a free pack that they could redeem in any supermarket, nationwide. An offer of a free cereal pack was of higher perceived value than a price reduction of 50p.

A 50p coupon would have cost the brand 30p and the retailer 20p. The free cereal promo cost the brand 10p per pack to fund and did not cost the retailer anything. This is because the number of consumers who value the offer buy the pack at the £3 but never end up claiming the free pack.

Kellogg has repeated these types of promotions because of their success at adding value without a price discount.

So where's the catch? Like all markets, brands are not used to having to think of packaging as a promotional medium. Not long ago a brand could develop a good product and simply advertise it using broadcast media like TV and radio. It is only recently that brands have realistically been able to contemplate having a direct relationship with their consumers. The cloud and digital database capability makes this possible.

The size of the opportunity is clear. Packaging can play a large role. Brands need to address how they use their packaging and unlock its hidden potential to work as a bona fide medium in its own right. This is easy to say, but it equates to a large difference in positioning. A big reframe for packaging is not something that can happen overnight.

Packaging professionals need to ask themselves, 'How committed are we to reframing and repositioning our role in our companies?

How will packaging be able to show its value and be understood?' Any change like this requires commitment, internal resources and a budget to engage professionals tasked with extracting more measurable brand building value from packaging.

> *Connecting with your consumer doesn't necessarily mean complex and expensive connected packaging. FMCG brands must unlock new ways to form legitimate and value-add relationships; embracing and leveraging solutions that infer intelligence and that help create a real bond with the user.*
>
> **Tom Lawrie-Fussey**
> Business Developer and Entrepreneur,
> Cambridge Design

Chapter 5

THE 6 RS METHODOLOGY

My methodology, entitled the 6 Rs Methodology, aims to provide six simple and practical rules to assess your packaging on its contribution and unlock the hidden value, ensuring packaging works hard for your brand.

When a brand is designing and developing its packaging, it has a lot of variables to wrestle with. So, no wonder that it often does not maximise the value packaging could deliver. Like most things in life, without a methodology – a habit – things don't happen.

Having completed several market campaigns with Hive, Ipackaging Expertise Ltd was founded to help brands benefit from what was learned. The 6 Rs Methodology does not attempt to cover any of the traditional roles of packaging. It has been designed to be an additional asset to your packaging design.

Let's say I have a pack design. If I want to extract the most value from it, what else can I do? Let's follow the 6 Rs Methodology and look at packaging from completely different perspectives:

- A media perspective
- A consumer relationship perspective
- A brand building perspective
- A direct sales driver perspective

Brands that do this will have a larger chance of success in the competitive market that we work in.

The first thing to investigate is how much value the brand will gain if its packaging can get consumers to:

- **React**, generating more sales through maximum reaction to packaging on the shop's shelf
- **Read** the message on pack
- **Respond** to the message on a pack and do something about it
- **Return,** generating more brand loyalty and sales by interacting with the pack every time they buy the product
- **Remember** the branded pack they buy
- **Recommend** the branded pack to their personal network

> *Packaging needs to be seen as a method to 'add value' and not just seen as a cost centre.*
>
> **Bruce Funnell**
> Head of Packaging, Nestlé York

Brands find it difficult to add a clear, measurable, tangible value to things they invest in to help them grow. For example, if a brand buys an advertisement, how many extra sales will it generate? What extra impact will it have on brand value? Equally there is a challenge for brands to correlate the value packaging can deliver towards extra sales, extra engagement, more brand value, stronger brand loyalty, brand equity and brand advocacy.

The 6 Rs explore the added value that a brand can gain from maximising each component.

React

Consumers don't spend a lot of time in the shop standing at the fixture where your pack is stocked. So, what are you doing to with your packaging to ensure the consumer reacts to it?

I'm sure all packaging designers will say they are maximising the pack's ability to get a customer to react to it and buy it, but there are several other factors they are forced to consider. They cannot just focus on the pack's ability to create a reaction. Alongside the usual things like holding the product through its distribution channels, communicating all the details about the product, etc, sometimes packs offer extra functions like helping in the cooking process or the dispensing process.

The ability of a pack to make a consumer react can be split into two parts:

- Consumer reaction factor at point of purchase
- Consumer reaction to the pack after they have purchased it

How good your pack design is can be judged against its ability to get a consumer to react. The ability of a pack to stimulate a reaction is measured as:

- Sales uplift when a pack is upgraded with a feature to increase the reaction factor, but often there are lots of other variables that affect the sales so this is not that accurate
- Dynamic surveys of consumers on the features that they notice on the pack

There are lots of things packaging designers can do with construction to encourage the consumer to react to the pack design. Look at the packaging of an iPhone or an Apple Mackintosh. It feels special, and the consumer makes a brand connection well before they have got to the product.

The Pringle round can is a good example of a pack construction that stands out by its shape. It's a great construction for point of purchase and after purchase. But what options are available to increase the Pringle can's ability to drive a reaction? Is its construction doing the most it can? Actually, there are lots more things the brand can do with the pack.

Let's look at a Pringle can's construction, looking at practical improvements first. The lid on the round tower could have different shapes, different colours, different textures. A round tower is good, but what about oval?

One good example of a construction design that improves the reaction factor is the M&S injection moulded oval soup drum, mentioned in Chapter 2. It has a large dimple in it, enticing consumers to hold the belly of the drum. Even though changing shape means investing in a new and expensive construction tool, a user friendly consumer shape is more likely to encourage the consumer to react to the pack.

There's potential for many more improvements to the internal construction for when a consumer has purchased the product. The Moreinside mechanic, created at Packaging Media Ltd, has shown that when the consumer opens the lid and sees the foil membrane they need to tear back to release the product, the brand can make use of the time while the consumer's opening the product or waiting for it to cook. What about a booklet that opens up when the consumer pulls back the membrane? That would get a reaction.

Once the consumer has opened the membrane, they could be enticed to look at its reverse to evoke another reaction. What about the base of the can? Would it be possible to add an innovative construction there?

A lot of time, money and effort is spent on designing the ability of a pack to drive a reaction at point of purchase. In my opinion, the design industry also needs to work hard on the pack design's ability to create a reaction after the consumer has purchased the product. There is not enough critical analysis of this.

Print is a huge area of potential, but brands compromise so much with the print design. Typically, cost limits how much a brand spends on the print specification. The value assigned to the pack's ability to stimulate a reaction is not measured accurately enough for the brand to understand the extra value obtainable, even with a higher cost.

Packaging Media showed that by simply investing in more expensive packaging, the packaging could justify itself from the added value it created. A great example of this was a campaign run for a range of Waitrose Chinese ready meals. The ready meal brand chose to upgrade the packaging to include a printed booklet that increased the cost of print by at least 10p per pack. £100,000 for every million packs.

The added cost was more than justified when the results of the campaign were analysed. Over 10% of their shoppers were not aware of the range of Chinese meals Waitrose offered. This booklet increased this awareness.

Very often brands compromise on:

- Colour
- Special varnishes – even a simple matt finish can make a huge difference to a pack's stand-out factor
- Foil blocking, which can include holography where the print design changes as the consumer looks at the pack from different angles
- Personalisation –a unique ID printed on the pack can increase its ability to create a reaction

The challenge in print is to create a reaction prior to purchase. But how can the print help create a reaction after purchase? That's the new industry challenge. Are there methods to use ink that changes colour in the fridge? The Coors Light bottle with a label that changes when the beer is at the right temperature gets a great reaction. What else? Are there clever interactive methods that will change designs with pressure?

Touch is a very important factor to drive a reaction. One of my first jobs was selling suits and high quality menswear with Jaeger London. In clothing retailing, the first thing salespeople learn is to get the customer to touch the fabric. The minute they feel the fabric quality, the customer is drawn to the product. In my early days with packaging garments, I soon discovered that the packaging that allowed a customer to touch the product was the winner.

Often, too little importance is placed on the feel of a pack substrate, and the price of the substrate is the key deciding factor. Touch can have such a strong pull on a consumer, creating a reaction both prior to and after purchase. Simple methods need to be explored. Brands need to ask, 'Does the feel of our packaging do as much as it could to create a reaction?' For example, plastic can be embossed. Textured plastic butter tubs would create a stronger reaction factor than smooth ones.

A good example of a brand using touch is Heineken in France with its glass bottles of beer. The brand intentionally came up with a form of glass that would get more scratched as it was reused. Because glass bottles are returned through the trade, Heineken's marketing has used the recycling of the glass in its favour.

Each bottle has a unique code on it. Customers are asked to log onto an app, enter the code and register as somebody who has drunk a glass of beer from the bottle. The history and the long-term value of the brand is reinforced using touch and a digital interface.

All beverage cans are currently smooth to the touch. Is there no one who wants a rough embossed image to create a different effect?

There are lots of innovative papers and boards on the market – ones that feel like rubber, natural paper, have a high tech touch, an environmental touch. However, most boards and papers use the same effect. Why do most labels feel the same to the touch? Is it simply that brands are not looking at the importance of touch in helping the pack get the consumer to react?

A new technique has been developed that enables carton suppliers to digitally die cut the board to pinpoint accuracy. Because the method does not need a conventional die cutting and stripping board, it can cut some ornate designs. Cleverly, the system makes people want to touch it.

Curiosity. In my early days, I had to do a fair amount of cold calling. I always remember calling a hard-nosed cockney who, being time poor, said that he had loads of cold calls and could not see why he should spend the time speaking to me.

So I said, 'I understand, but don't forget that curiosity killed the cat.' I challenged him to call me back if he was curious as to whether I could help.

He rang me back the next morning and said, 'You are right, I am curious. What have you got for me?'

Packaging media using a serrated zipper-like construction with a little arrow die cut into the board leads the consumer to want to tear the zipper and discover something new. It creates curiosity, getting the consumer to react to the pack. Often saying nothing but enticing the consumer to reveal more helps increase the appeal of the pack.

Visit my website www.turakhia.co.uk to see some tear off mechanic models branded as Moreinside.

Read

One of packaging's core challenges is to encourage the consumer to read it. Packaging can be judged by how enticing it is to read.

Consumers read the packaging to understand what the product contains or how to use it. Packaging needs to work harder and assess itself on its ability to get a consumer to read more than just the bare essentials. It needs to ask itself,

> **'Am I being used as much as I could to get a consumer to connect enough to read something on me?'**

When they're assessed against this criteria, most packs are under-performing dramatically.

Think about it like a newspaper. If a reader buys a newspaper every day to look at the sports section and the weather, the rest of the paper has to work really hard to get them to read other articles in it.

Something enticing for the customer to read about the brand is a powerful medium. Growing the strength of consumer relationships is the foundation of brand success. Print media like magazine and newspaper advertisements or even a door drop are all based on the power of getting a consumer to read text and look at images.

On top of designing a pack to carry enough information, brands need to assess their packaging's ability to entice the consumer to read something more. Each pack can be regarded as a method to get the consumer to connect with the brand.

Innocent is a brand that used text on the pack as an engaging vehicle very well. Simple, quirky jokes were cleverly positioned on the carton, and consumers learnt to look for them.

Cobra Beer is a great example of packaging being used to stimulate a consumer's desire to read. The glass bottle is embossed with a story of Karan Bilimoria, the founder of Cobra and a man with a mission. It uses touch to drive curiosity.

If a pack designer needs to design a pack which introduces more space to include text/imagery that the consumer can read, what is restricting them? Typically, it is the amount of legal text that the packaging designer already has to fit on the pack. Usually designers are space poor, so they don't even consider the idea of finding more space on the pack to add more text. A packaging designer needs to be tasked with the job of developing a pack that has sufficient space for standard text to describe product and meet legal requirements, and extra space to entice consumers to read more about the brand. Here are some simple suggestions as to how they can do that.

Board packaging options. A board carton can find more print space by printing on the inside of the box. However, the issue with this is that the consumer is reluctant to destroy the box to read the inside. Instead, a simple leaflet inserted in the box provides an easier and more effective solution. Back in our Packaging Media Ltd days, we discovered that a separate printed leaflet in a box got a good response.

Discovery Foods produced a kit box for the consumer to make up Mexican products like fajtas. When they ran a promotion, they inserted a separate leaflet into the box that was revealed by the consumer when they unpacked the kit box to make their fajitas. The response rates for this campaign far exceeded comparative campaigns where the promotion was on the box. A separate inserted booklet in a pack of dry petfood by Pedigree Petfoods resulted in an impressive response rate of over 14%.

Stealing a piece of the conventional print to incorporate a section for promotional text is possible, but because the main part of the print is telling consumers about the product, using another part of the box for a different message has limited impact. The pack is communicating two messages that are competing against each other.

Moreinside is a system for branded packaging that was designed to add extra pieces of print as effective media and use the pack as a carrier. If you look at the ready meal examples on my website, Turakhia.co.uk, you will see systems that allow a pack to have an extra piece of print for consumers to read without compromising the main roles of the packs.

The picture below shows a real example of using a board ready meal sleeve to entice a consumer to read an independent piece of print.

WAITROSE CHINESE READY MEAL SLEEVE

OUTSIDE OF JACKET: MIRRORS BOX DESIGN

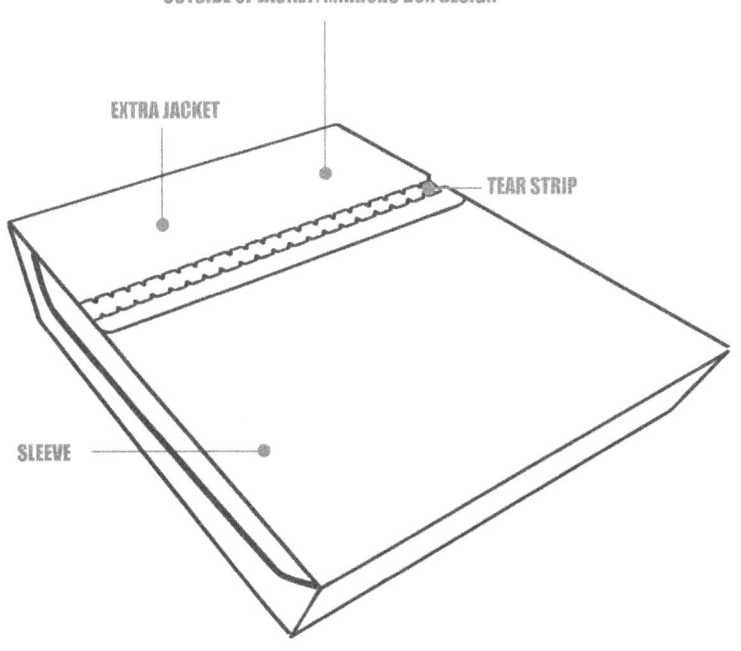

EXTRA JACKET

TEAR STRIP

SLEEVE

If Packaging Could Talk

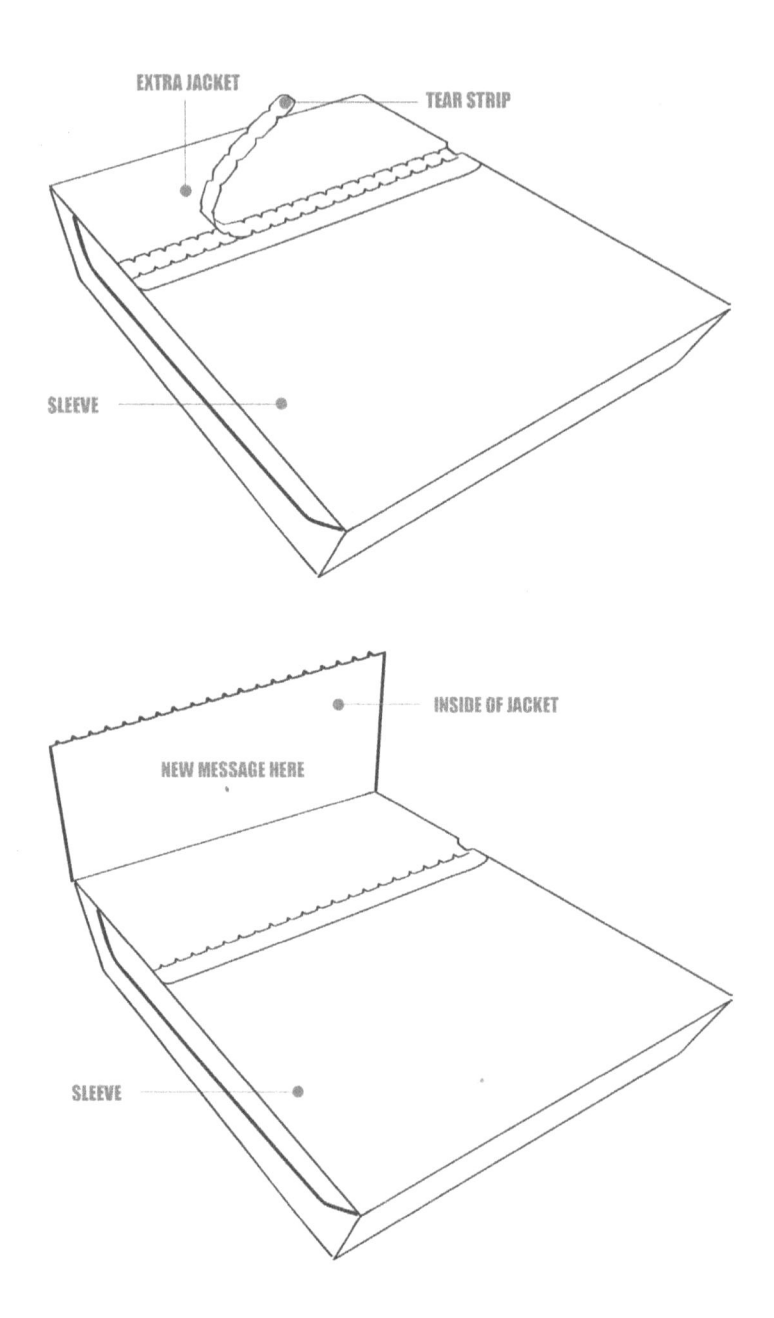

EXTRA JACKET
TEAR STRIP
SLEEVE

INSIDE OF JACKET
NEW MESSAGE HERE
SLEEVE

The outside of the pack communicates the brand and the meal it packs. But the pack is a part of a large range of Waitrose Chinese meals. Waitrose wants to communicate its offering as a bona fide replacement for a Chinese takeaway.

The board sleeve has a sticker on it that entices the consumer to tear it off. When torn, the sticker reveals a folded piece of print that can neatly carry an independent message. The leaflet includes a picture of a table full of the whole appetising range of Waitrose Chinese meals, showing the depth of the Waitrose Chinese experience. It even suggests a good beer to drink with it, and carries a money off coupon for this beer. This engaging technique brings the brand message across to the consumer, reaching them at the right time. A traditional ready meal sleeve would be read for the cooking instructions and then thrown away.

Packaging's ability to get a separate piece of print to a consumer has clear advantages when compared with a traditional medium like door dropping. First and foremost, there's cost. Door dropping directly to a consumer's household would cost circa six or seven times more than distributing print on packaging. Secondly, door dropping media tends to come through the consumer's letterbox uninvited. The packaging media model works on the basis that the consumer has already chosen to buy the product and so is likely to be curious enough to reveal and read the concealed leaflet.

Bighams is a great brand. It makes premium ready meals that are genuinely restaurant standard. Bighams has incorporated a flap similar to Packaging Media's Sleeve Media. It encourages the consumer to read the contents by simply moving the flap that protrudes from the packaging. The flap is always on the pack, and not just when there is a promotion, so the pack is driving a habit to incentivise the consumers to read it.

Every pack with a label could carry a booklet. Why not? Why spend money on media trying to get a consumer to read an advertisement when you can use your pack to carry messages? Simply buy more print space and then get the creative teams to give the consumers a reason to tear and reveal the print. Use a curiosity mechanic to get the consumers wanting to read the booklets.

Separate the design process by asking if your brand's packaging mechanic is driving the consumer to be curious enough to reveal the message. Is the message enticing enough?

Packaging designers need to work on the packaging mechanic. Creative marketing teams need to know their audiences well enough to get their consumers to want to read the extra piece of print. Both need to work in tandem.

Anchor Butter uses a membrane that the consumer has to tear off to access the butter. Our company ran the reward scheme for this campaign and the redemption levels were strong. A strong reason for this was because Anchor used an independent piece of packaging to print a message.

Even flexible packs can have systems to add extra areas of print. Simply inserting flow wrapped pieces of print in a bag of crisps or sweets can have a huge effect on the pack's readability.

If brands take up the challenge to entice their consumers to look to their packaging for something to read, then they need to plan to make this habitual. Consumers will then actively look for the extra print material. Some brands already use their packaging areas as a print medium to communicate a message, but often it is only when they have something to say. Because it is not an ongoing packaging strategy, its potential is heavily underexploited. If the packaging does not usually have an extra print area, consumers don't expect it and hence it has little value. The value needs to be recognised, and this only happens if the consumers are committed to extracting it.

Ask your packaging designers and suppliers to use systems like Moreinside that release independent pieces of valuable print.

There are no technological limitations to making packaging offer much more print space for consumers to read. When brands understand the media value of packaging, they can treat it like their own magazine.

Respond

OK, you have a pack that gets a consumer to react before purchase and after, and ignites their curiosity so they read all the print on it and concealed within it. But packaging needs to measure itself on more than this.

Will a consumer *respond* to the pack?

There are simple methods to assess packaging's ability to get consumers to respond to its messages. Obviously, the consumer's interest needs to be engaged enough before a brand can ask them to respond, as without relevance and interest a consumer won't respond. However, the packaging format used also has a vital role to play. The better the packaging mechanic, the more likely it is that the consumer will respond to the message.

Digital technology has provided easy methods for brands to ask their consumers to respond via their packaging:

- Register online using the packaging URL link
- Download an app
- Tap the pack if your smartphone carries NFC and you have an Android phone

- Enter a pack ID, a unique code from the pack
- Scan a pack ID

Packaging designers need to create packaging that leads to the best response. It goes without saying that packaging formats and creativity lead to consumer engagement. The acid test is, has the packaging format led to a response?

The best example I have seen of a packaging mechanic designed to get a response was the Yoplait promotion.

Yoplait, a yoghurt company, was running an on-pack promotion. To get a response, the pack could be converted into pair of glasses with red lenses. Mums were invited to encourage their children to cut out the glasses and look at a character on the back of the pack. Only with the glasses could the children read what was under the character as the print appeared blurred otherwise. Under the character was a code that the children could enter online to win *Minions* prizes.

Packaging is used in promotions to drive consumer response The Moreinside system we introduced on ready meal sleeves was easy to implement and had a very small additional on-cost.

The Tesco ready meal sleeve, by using a longer piece of board, was able to carry two independent pieces of print that the consumer tore to reveal. This was powerful additional print. It enticed consumers to reveal the extra information, and carried a very low on-cost – less than 2% of the cost of a postage stamp.

In getting the packaging right, brands have to give consumers tangible reasons to want to engage and respond to the pack. Brands need ways to stay close to their consumers so that they can understand what engages them and hence justify asking them to develop a closer relationship.

Traditionally brands have tried to understand consumers by aggregated data, trends on behaviour, etc. This is no longer accurate or personal enough. Brands need to provide consumers with reasons to opt in to communication from them, either by email or through an App, or using new technology. This ensures that they know their consumers well enough to provide enticing messages.

If a consumer is going to respond to a brand's message, the pack needs two things: a clever packaging mechanic that drives the consumer to want to reveal and read it, and a clever engagement message that drives the consumer to respond.

In the UK, people get obsessed with the weather. A brand promotion was created where consumers purchased a snack food brand and entered a code, and then they could pick the area of the UK where they believed it would rain next. If they got it right, they would win a prize. This content was highly engaging and got a large number of the UK population participating. It also triggered lots of free press due to the subject matter.

Creative promotional departments and consumer insight experts spend lots of resources on engagement, working out reasons for a consumer to respond. The way for every promotion to attract a consumer's attention is to focus on the packaging format. Look for one that stands out, gives the message on an independent piece of print, and clearly distinguishes this message from the normal packaging information.

Packaging formats need to be tried and tested against the response levels for a promotion. All too often, the only thing measured is the promotion's creative element. From experience, I can confirm that highly relevant and valuable brand communication can be lost if the packaging mechanic used does not stimulate a response.

We ran a promotion on a salad bag that offered a free bottle of wine in return for the purchase of three of the bags. The salad bags cost £1.50 each, and the wine would normally cost £6 a bottle so it was a worthwhile offer, but the message was poorly designed and the basic packaging was used to communicate the offer. This led to a very poor response even for such a strong offer.

A consumer needs to respond to the pack whatever the promotion, so brands need to give much more attention to measuring the packaging mechanic and its ability to drive a response. If the response element of the packaging is measured, then brands have a lot of scope to design even cleverer packaging to help build further response. Usually the vital ingredient is the packaging mechanic. Measuring the response element of packaging will ensure that it can work harder than ever.

Return

Once a brand has made one connection with a consumer, will that consumer return, and why?

When the pack has got a consumer to react to it, read it and respond to it, has it done its job? Actually, the pack has only just started.

Brands spend lots of time trying to get a consumer to buy their products once. A single purchase can be defined as a connection. What does the pack have to do if the brand wishes to develop a bond with the consumer strong enough to ensure the consumer moves from a connection to a relationship?

How can packs get a consumer to return to the brand?

Packs need to carry a reason for consumers to value them and recognise that each one has its own secret value, even if it initially looks exactly like the previous pack the consumer purchased. So, each pack needs to have a unique element; a unique reason for the consumer to return. This is where unique codes come into their own.

It becomes a bit like a passport. The pack carries its own unique ID for its entire life cycle.

If the brand emphasises the fact that the packaging is unique within its promotional messaging, then the pack can build a much stronger relationship with a consumer. A consumer who has scrutinised the branded pack after the initial purchase in order to find the unique code will be far more likely to remember the pack design, the brand it represents, and build a bond. Unique codes or unique pack IDs give packaging a return factor – a real reason for the consumer to engage with the pack. Brands can then measure the number of times a consumer has connected with the brand by measuring the number of pack IDs they've entered.

If a promotion involves the consumer needing just one pack and one pack ID, then the pack gets just one chance to gain the consumer's attention. If the consumer returns to the pack for a code, each visit encourages them to get more familiar with the branded pack they have purchased. Its value increases significantly. A direct correlation can be made between brand to consumer relationship strength and the number of times a consumer has connected with the pack.

Packs that get consumers to return to the brand and engage with it can contribute more directly to building brand equity. They assist brand building through direct connections between the pack and the consumer.

A snack food brand in the UK ran an amazing promotion that used packs with a strong return element, each carrying a unique pack ID.

The promotion was described as a holiday give-away. The creative element, however, was extremely engaging, using a simple Scrabble-type gaming concept. Consumers entered codes from packs and each code gave them a letter. The digital interface allowed them to work up the letters on a Scrabble-type board to spell out the name of a holiday destination. Consumers quickly amassed most of the letters and then got a real bug to find their missing letter. They could also swap letters with other consumers. Participation figures were huge.

Code based promotions are ones where the brand wants to use the code as a secure proof of purchase – ie, the consumer has to buy product and proves they have done so by entering the code. Typically, promotions ask the consumer to enter one code or two during the promotion. Some successful ones, like the Kellogg's 'collect for a free spoon' or 'claim a free pack', can get the consumer to buy three packs to obtain three codes and participate by entering these all three codes. Defining a promotion that can get the consumer to want to collect more than three codes and thus have to buy more than three packs of any product is much more of a challenge. This promotion managed to get an average of not three codes per consumer, but over twenty-nine. Furthermore, this statistic is only an average. Over 90,000 consumers entered between 100 and 500 codes each, in just six weeks!

The promotion was a success when measured in terms of sales uplift, and the packs' contribution to increasing the brand's equity speaks out loud and clear. A promotion that gets a consumer to purchase twenty-nine packs and interact with the brand twenty-nine times must have significantly added brand equity value. To participate in the promotion, the consumer had to recognise the branded pack instore, look at the pack to take the unique code from it, and enter the code on a branded site.

One can safely say that the consumers who entered twenty-nine codes would be able to recognise the pack design and know the brand to which it belonged.

Packs should strive to give consumers reasons to choose the same brand next time they shop. Promotions are fine, but if brands commit to measuring themselves *generally* on whether consumers return to them, I am sure their creative departments will come up with exciting ideas. The key is to measure the pack on its ability to get a consumer to return to it, and the rest should follow.

A vital step for packaging is to make it unique. Companies like Hive IP make it practical and factory-friendly for every pack to have a unique ID on it all of the time.

Digital printing is growing as an option. It is estimated that mainstream packaging converters like corrugated manufacturers and flexible film printers will be able to supply mainstream packaging requirements using digital technology in fewer than five years. Digital printing can not only allocate a unique ID to every pack, but can give every pack a unique design.

Why would brands not prioritise the need for digital personalisation of their packs? Two simple reasons:

- They don't measure packs by their ability to get a consumer to return to the brand
- They don't have financial modelling of the impact on brand-value that packs can have if

> they encourage consumers to return to the brand multiple times

Here are a few examples of branded packs that get a consumer to return to them after purchase.

The McDonald's coffee cup is a great example. The brand runs a promotion that offers a free coffee for every five cups the consumer buys. The method for consumers to collect for their free coffee could have involved a mechanic independent of the packaging. However, McDonald's attaches media value to its coffee cups, even though they are disposable. The brand incorporated a collector card into the coffee cup that consumers tear off. A peelable sticker, which acts as a proof of purchase, is attached to the card each time the consumer buys a coffee. When the card has five stickers on it, the consumer can hand it into the McDonald's outlet to claim their free coffee.

This example drives home the power of using the pack itself as the reason to return. The collector card that the consumer can tear off is on every cup, constantly reminding the consumer of the added value of the McDonald's cup. Any other coffee cup has much less value. Consumers just see it as a means to an end.

The other learning from this scheme is the longevity in the programme. All McDonald's cups have this system on them and have used it for years. Consumers are habitual creatures, and the McDonald's coffee cup has given them a long-term reason to remain loyal using a clever packaging mechanic and promotion.

Yeo Valley is an interesting example to mention. This dairy brand markets its yoghurts in a packaging format that is a plastic cup covered with a board jacket. The board jacket is only glued down one line on the cup, and so consumers can tear a serrated cutter profile and reveal the inside of the jacket, which can carry print. Yeo Valley recognised the value of this print and often uses it to distribute messages.

Remember

Will consumers remember your packaging?

Brands may argue that packaging's job has always involved getting the consumer to remember it. Yes, it has. But the boundaries of 'me too' brands are very narrow. 'Me too' brands make their packaging look so similar to a respected brand's design that it is not so easy for the consumer to remember the original packaging.

The measurement of 'remember' is that the consumer needs to remember a brand's packaging well enough for them to select the branded pack when they revisit a crowded retail space where there are lots of similar designs. They must remember the pack to be able to choose it.

Packaging is trying hard to make itself so clearly differentiated that the consumer will remember it. There are lots of great examples of packaging that has succeeded in this endeavour. Several have been mentioned in this book.

However, brands need to measure this success, proactively monitoring it on an ongoing basis. They need to ask,

'How is our packaging doing with respect to whether consumers are remembering it?'

The first requirement is to recognise the need for your brand's packaging to be remembered, and to measure against this criteria for a lot longer than just after the package has been designed. The value of a pack is directly related to its ability to be remembered.

We mention the McDonald's coffee cups. But what about a Costa Coffee cup, where the jacket around the cup is fluted corrugated? Sure, this will be a strong feature that the brand will be remembered for... until a competitor launches cups using the same design. Remembering the packaging is one thing, but the memory must be related to the brand. The consumer needs to remember the corrugated coffee cup as a Costa model.

I must admit, I have not heard of brands assessing their packaging on its ability to be remembered. My first piece of advice would be for brands to incorporate an annual or biannual measurement metric to quantify the ability of consumers to remember their packaging design, e.g. surveys of a customer base with a benchmark. Different features can then be added to the pack and measured on their ability to drive the pack's ability to be remembered. Very small changes to packaging often have a significant impact.

I always remember a clever packaging mechanic used by an Australian wine brand called Oxford Landing. The brand used a straightforward bottle with a mainstream bottle shape, a screw-on top and two labels, one front and one back – a standard packaging style that most New World brands were using. What Oxford Landing did differently was to include a perforation on the back label. By selectively leaving glue-free areas, the brand was able to invite the consumer to tear off little squares of paper from the label on which the brand name 'Oxford Landing' was printed. The statement on the pack said 'To remember the wine you drank, tear this and keep'.

Clever. By making the consumer recognise that they may well forget the brand they had just drunk, inviting them to tear a piece of print off the bottle that they could keep in their purse or wallet, Oxford Landing knew that consumers would remember the bottle of wine they'd enjoyed. Even if they didn't tear the label off, the invitation to do so triggered a better memory of the brand than if the bottle had just had a standard bottle label on it. A good example of the pack giving the consumer something to remember.

Every packaging designer or marketer needs to ask, 'What is it that will make consumers remember my pack?' They need to incorporate something into the design feature to drive a customer to remember it. Brands need to measure the pack's ability to get a consumer to remember it and understand the value added if a consumer does so. They can subsequently make this measurement a tangible value that they can justify the cost of packaging against.

Recommend

Now the ultimate test: can packaging get a recommendation? What can the packaging do to get consumers recommending its brand?

Recommendation requires a consumer to admire the pack enough and trust the product enough to mention it to somebody they know. No one likes to recommend something unless they are 100% sure that they are giving value and their referral will live up to the expectation they have created.

The value of recommendation is huge. Social media has shown that if a person likes something, shares it and recommends it to their friends, they can generate momentum and a large following quite quickly.

I was privileged to work for a successful restaurant entrepreneur called Bob Payton in the 80s. Bob's first success was bringing Chicago deep dish pizza to London. I remember asking him the secret behind his success.

He answered, 'Not advertising!'

Ironically, Bob was an advertising specialist prior to his move into the restaurant business. He explained to me why he felt a restaurant should not need advertising. Successful restaurants grow with personal referrals and recommendations.

He explained, 'Son, my first restaurant, The Chicago Pizza Factory, was in a location difficult to find, and one that would

The 6 Rs Methodology

not generate any passing trade. People had to make a conscious decision to come for my pizza. I made sure that we made the best deep dish pizza one could imagine.

'The first six months were extremely slow, so I invited friends and family. The next six months were still slow, but I had one essential ingredient: recommendation. Everyone who tasted my pizza went out of their way to recommend my restaurant and explain how to find it.'

The Chicago Pizza Factory was a huge success, and after a year, diners could rarely get a table on arrival. The restaurant took no reservations, but had a cocktail bar for diners to spend their money in while waiting for a table.

The one restaurant concept that Bob Payton launched that he had to advertise was a flop and he closed it down.

Brands need to re-evaluate the basics:

- Get a consumer to buy the product
- Encourage the consumer to recommend it to others
- Repeat the process

Packaging has a vital role in making sure consumers recommend a product. In fact, the packaging can often be the main reason consumers decide to recommend. Here are some recommendations packaging can drive:

'Those packs always have a unique code on them.' If the pack can get a consumer to respond to it by visiting a website, registering their details and entering a pack code, then it is doing well. The power of data then needs to work hard to engage the consumer so that they recommend the brand. The packaging mechanic is the first step to this recommendation.

'That pack is great, so easy to use.' A pack that gives good functionality is an easy method to drive referral, but one that drives recommendation has to be *remarkably* good. Some products are more likely to suit this than others, eg ring pulls on cans or resealable mini grips on bags.

The Ella's Kitchen pack, which allows consumers to eat mushy fruit directly from it, is a good example of a pack with a distinctive enough functionality to drive referral. Single serve cat food pouches and cardboard pots to make up instant porridge are also good examples, and Walkers will be hoping the new 'Tear and Share' pack will encourage consumers to recommend it as a great pack style when entertaining.

Pack personalisation is a potential method to drive recommendation. The Coke campaign with named bottles was designed for consumers to show off to their friends. If they found a Coke bottle with their name on it, they could share the experience on social media. Because packs were personalised, consumers sought them out then recommended them with shares when they found their own name.

Digital print means that personalisation can be pushed further. Imagine a carton with a limited edition of different art prints. When consumers have purchased a pack showing a print that they like, they will talk about it and recommend the brand to others.

There are different print technologies available that can help a pack generate a recommendation. The first step needs to be measure and assess pack designs against their ability to drive a recommendation, allocating financial value to this. Hotel Chocolat is a good example of this where consumers could easily state, 'Hotel Chococlat is great, good packaging design'. Twinings Tea packs won awards from their packaging getting consumers to say, 'The Twinings packaging is great'.

Improved product usage. If the pack can enhance consumers' experiences when they're using a brand then it is likely to drive a recommendation. The Coors Light beer bottle is a good example, where the pack label changes colour when the beer bottle is chilled to the ideal serving temperature. That is pretty 'cool'.

There are lots of different ways that packs can help consumers drive a recommendation. Even the graphics can get results. Being into print and packaging, I often recommend a pack on its design, eg, 'The Kettle Chips pack is really compelling, have you seen it?'

Getting a pack to generate a consumer recommendation is not easy. Some may argue that it is too optimistic to even try, but I believe the value of a consumer referral in FMCG is not separated out enough or properly pared down to packaging's contribution to driving this effect.

Packaging has a lot to offer and is all too often being underutilised. The untapped role it has is its media's capability to develop multiple direct and close relationships between it and the consumer. It needs to be seen as a bona fide medium in its own right.

Packaging needs to measure itself against the 6 Rs and consistently look to improve these measurements. Any packaging converter looking to encourage the market to increase packaging's profile will need to recognise the 6 Rs as benchmarks against which branded packaging can be designed to deliver. There needs to be a clear commercial value assigned to each R so as to justify the incremental cost vs value argument when designing packaging features.

Without clear metrics and correlation of the brand-building value packaging has, brands will continue to under-utilise this asset. Packaging heads have an ideal opportunity to enhance the role packaging plays in helping to build the brand.

To summarise, brands need to evaluate their packaging against the 6 Rs:

- React
- Read
- Respond
- Return
- Remember
- Recommend

Then they can come up with ways to assess their packs' performance against these 6 Rs, ensuring they work on financial modelling to ascertain the value for each R.

In your company, make this a habit. Use professionals like Ipackaging Expertise to help implement structured ways to reframe packaging and packaging's contribution.

Raising the bar for packaging. The challenge is in the implementation.

Chapter 6

IMPLEMENTATION

Packaging has a lot on its plate. Changing the way brands look at their packaging and the demands they put on it to contribute more cannot be done overnight. The 6 Rs are an ambitious measurement criteria.

So how can brands unwrap the untapped value of packaging for brand success? They need three things:

1. **Commitment.** Nothing really happens without commitment. You get what you commit to. Brands need to commit to a process to change.

2. **Resource.** An internal resource will need to be allocated to the exercise.

3. **Budget.** The most efficient method to drive change is to commission specialists to make the change happen. Companies like Ipackaging Expertise will take you through the following stepped process.

Step 1: internal value metrics

Brands all value things differently, and offline FMCG brands have a real challenge in translating value from their expenses. Getting an ROI is high on most FMCG brands' agendas. That said, many brands don't have clear ROI models, and often it is difficult to get straight answers without questioning or data mining across the organisation.

So step 1 is to define value. How does a brand value media? How are its budgets compiled? For example, a brand may spend £X million a year on TV advertising. Does this translate to sales? How? Is it to do with consumer engagement?

If packaging is to be seen as a true medium, how will its impact be measured? Will there be budget available if these metrics are met? Often brands say they value something but will not be able to invest in it as it does not fit into their budgetary exercise. This is a challenge. Aligning budgets and value takes time and consultation with a variety of stakeholders, but must be done before brands can make progress.

Step 2: agreeing yardsticks

Having understood how value could be measured in the organisation, a brand needs to agree yardsticks that will be accepted by key stakeholders within the organisation. For example: 'If we spend £100,000 extra on the packaging, we will be happy if we could show that it extracted a database of consumers who had an annual value to us of £x.' Brand engagement can be measured by this method.

Companies need to define metrics that make sense internally and can show if the medium they are testing is better or worse than current models. This challenge cannot be underestimated. You can't really manage anything if you can't measure it, and so it is absolutely vital to agree clear measurement yardsticks.

Step 3: assess packaging

Having determined some targets, brands need to look at the packaging and consider mechanical options that could provide an independent media function. It's likely that there will be practical alternative methods that could be used with the factory filling machines. For example, a booklet label with a watch collar strap (a label shaped like a watch with a round centre and a strap on both sides) could be a neat method to make a labelled bottle have Moreinside. If the factory packing machine and label applicator cannot cope with the watch collar and the label thickness, then this will be impractical. However, if the financial metrics show that the medium will provide significant value, it may be worth investing in new label application machinery. Clear understanding of the cost vs value model is the key.

Step 4: pilot study test

Agree to run a pilot test with clear measurement metrics against which to assess. Coordinate the test and assess the results. See if the results can be translated back into the agreed measurement metrics.

Communicate the results back to the key stakeholders for their comments.

Step 5: implement

Decide whether the pilot tests indicate that the independent media function should be rolled into all the packaging or if a more scalable adoption should be taken. Agree yardsticks that suit the business internally.

Step 6: ongoing assessment

Assess the improvements annually with new technology options and new yardsticks. Such reviews are essential for management of a cultural change. All too easily, the brand will revert back to seeing packaging as it has done traditionally. Change management is hard work and requires a long-term commitment.

We have looked at packaging, analysing how it has powerful assets that brands can exploit more. We have demonstrated this value through real proof. We have introduced a methodology to design, measure and improve packaging so that it helps build the brand's ability to sell more and gain stronger relationships and connections with its end consumers.

Market for FMCG brands

The FMCG market will continue to be fiercely competitive. Brands will find it increasingly difficult to win a consumer's attention. Traditional retailing will change. Groceries could well all be delivered directly to your door.

Ad-blocking is already a big subject with 30% of consumers using an ad-blocker. Consumers will have more control and ownership of what messaging they accept, so reaching them will be much more difficult. The power of one retailer will be diluted as consumers will be choosing from a bigger variety of channels. Brands will have to work harder to gain custom and retain it.

There will be more and more pressure for packaging to increase its contribution in helping build the brand.

Now for a bit of fun. Where is packaging going? What will be different about packaging in ten years? Will it be similar to today? How will it change?

Personalised print. Digital print is coming. This will mean that pack designs will change more regularly and could become much more personalised to suit the time, season and consumer.

The more relevant and personal a pack can become, the more it will engage a consumer. The challenge to this industry will be to find ways to translate the power of new technology to real pounds, shillings and pence. Showing brands how digital print can help them to achieve their main goals will be the key for them to extract value from this powerful technology.

Connectivity. Most packs will be connected to the digital age, depending on what the brand can afford. Packs will be able to signal when a product is no longer suitable to be consumed. Some packaging will contain electronic devices that link to the web. Effectively, packs will give the consumer access to digital content through their devices. In purchasing the packs, they will access free content on the product simply by speaking.

Different packs will connect the consumer to different things. Packs might connect to a video, an augmented reality 3D experience, a piece of exclusive content, special offers on related products or repeat purchases of the same products. Sophisticated data techniques will be used to provide things that are relevant and engaging for the consumer to enjoy. A pack could be described as the portal to a world of digital content, accessible through purchase

Imagine buying a pack of fish and being able to tap it and access voice instructions on how to cook it, what to serve it with, which wine goes best with it, how it was caught and where the fish came from. Maybe even a promotional offer for your next purchase.

Personal DNA. Packs will all carry a unique identifiable code. This will be either integrated in an electronic chip such as an NFC chip or an alphanumeric or scannable code. This will mean consumers can electronically purchase a product and pay for it automatically. There will be an adoption curve of brands which use unique pack IDs. The brands will have the option to start with simple alphanumeric codes that can be entered on the web or smartphone. Then they might upgrade to a scannable code or digital printing solution, which will become available as the cost for electronic tags on packs comes down.

Lifestyle. FMCG brands will go through a complete reengineering of what their brands stand for. Are they merely products or do they associate themselves with consumers' lifestyles? Is a pizza a pizza, or is it a lads' night watching the football? A girlie night in? A Friday night romantic dinner? Consumers will then associate the product with the whole experience.

Nestlé is a fantastic example of how a brand can be completely reengineered. Ten years ago, Nescafé was Nestlé's coffee brand. Now the prime site location off Leicester Square, London is for Nespresso, Nescafé's coffee experience. It's not a shop, just a brand positioning like an expensive designer label. Consequently, Nestlé coffee is regarded as a private moment of luxury, the best thing consumers do in the day. Those lovely sharing moments.

Nespresso has nailed the experience value of coffee. So, what has this meant for packaging? Nespresso's packaging is premium. Compared to a jar, no expense has been spared. It's packed like an upmarket perfume or range of chocolates. Premium packaging that reflects the experience.

How will Nespresso's packaging need to develop? It will need to grow its ability to connect with the consumer and portray things aligned with the experience. It will possibly have intelligent ways of using electronic chips or NFC codes to take consumers to exclusive content that brings across the brand's lifestyle. It may look to incorporate clever packaging technologies that can automatically re-order when the pod flavour is running out. It may include more print media and automatic links to digital videos and sound to bring across what Nespresso stands for.

As other grocery products move into the 'product experience' model, so their packaging will have to follow suit. Will a bottle of wine deliver other things that go well with a girlie night in, like a DVD, snacks, a concert download. Will butchers attach themselves to the entertaining experience and deliver quality meat that they send with a butcher to cut the meat in front of the guests, and prepare the meat and a sauce, and serve?

There is a lot of work for brands to do to re-engineer their products around the experience they accompany, and packaging will have a vital role to play.

CONCLUSION

Packaging has a large scope to grow the value it provides to brands. But will it change?

If I look back over the last ten years, I am disappointed at how slowly packaging has evolved. There are not any significant changes to packaging that jump out at me. Why is this?

Airline ticket prices would never have changed if it hadn't been for easyJet disrupting the way companies sold seats on planes. Accommodation for visitors would have stayed the same if it hadn't been for Airbnb looking at a disruptive model to change the landscape. The way we listen to music would never have changed if it hadn't been for models like Spotify and streaming coming along.

What is it that packaging needs? The industry is full of groundbreaking technology. It simply needs a different way of looking at itself. Different yardsticks, different methodologies. Packaging is a tangible, physical medium, and has the ability to become a valuable digital medium.

It will be a great shame if packaging does not raise its game. It will need to follow the 6 Rs: drive a *reaction*; make a consumer *read* it, generate a *response*, *return* to it, *remember* it and *recommend* it.

It's a hard ask, but nothing that packaging cannot deliver if it puts its mind to it.

If not me, then who? If not now, when?

Mikhail Gorbachev

ACKNOWLEDGEMENTS

This book is dedicated to the world of packaging professionals and marketers, brand builders – anyone involved with driving brand growth primary packaging. I would like to mention and thank a few people without whom this book would not have been possible:

- Kyle Turakhia, Cambridge qualified English student, my youngest son, for editing the book cover to cover.

- Paul George, my lifelong designer. Designer of all the illustrations in this book.

- My parents for funding my education and teaching me how to live freely

- My father for his passion for entrepreneurialism

- John Robinson, founder of Southernhay Ltd, who ignited my interest in packaging

- André Wilkins of the Wilkins Print Group for his unlimited energy for carton printing and business

- Steli Hagi-Ioannou of easyJet for demonstrating the power and value of lateral thinking

- Rachel Swann, my business partner, for being brilliant

- Peter Burns of Waitrose, who backed the packaging media model

- Merric Mercer, my business partner, for his acumen and razor sharp logic
- Jonathan Jackson, my business partner, for his focus and relationship skills
- Ian Boulton and Paul Flynn for being real entrepreneurs
- Duncan Lowe for his friendship
- Rebecca Pierce, my coach, for professional life training and science
- My two boys Sachin and Kyle who continue to inspire me and teach me new life skills
- My mother for being my mum and giving me unconditional love
- My ex-wife, Caroline, for all her love, care and giving me two wonderful sons
- Steve Oldfield for being my best buddy and never doubting my literacy skills
- Teena Ackary for her kindness and love
- Daniel Priestley's KPI programme for providing a framework to ensure I 'write a book' as well as clarify the value proposition packaging has for the market

ABOUT THE AUTHOR

Keran Turakhia is from a well known Gujurati family, famous for bringing injection moulded plastic umbrella handles to the Indian market. Born with an Indian industrialist father and an eccentric, beautiful half-Swiss half-English mother, Keran was brought up in Bombay, now Mumbai, and sent to an English boarding school in Ooty, a hill station in Tamil Nadu. Keran completed his education in an International Centre in Sevenoaks, England, and qualified with a joint Chemical Engineering and Management honours degree from Loughborough University.

Being of an entrepreneurial family, Keran found his career in small business and management and has been in packaging all his life. Given his multicultural background, he has always been a change agent. He has run a small trade finishing business, sold primary packaging to a variety of European countries. He won the Queen's Award for Export for creating an export business for Robinsons of Chesterfield, a spiral wound round packaging supplier (a decorated toilet roll). He was the first to introduce printed plastic as an alternative to printed board packaging into the mass food ready-meal market – an extraordinary achievement given the fact that plastic was at least five times more expensive than printed board. More recently he has focussed on Intelligent

Packaging and how to increase packaging's contribution towards brand health. He has the rare expertise of knowing how mass market FMCG/CPG brands can benefit from linking their products to the digital age and giving every pack a unique pack ID.

He has large shareholdings in three B2B companies now: Different Packaging Ltd, Ipackaging Expertse Ltd and Hive IP Ltd. He loves to celebrate life's every moment and has more recently set up a company called Samosa Wallah Ltd. A B2C business focusing on serving freshly fried hot samosas to the public with a smile.

You can find out more, or get in touch with Keran at:
www.turakhia.co.uk
www.ipackagingexpertise.com
www.differentpackaging.co.uk

@KeranTurakhia
KeranTurakhia

CPSIA information can be obtained
at www.ICGtesting.com
Printed in the USA
LVHW051051050121
675771LV00023B/890